BIG-NOTE PIANO

CLASSIC MOTOWN

ISBN 0-634-00014-4

HAL•LEONARD® CORPORATION
7777 W. BLUEMOUND RD. P.O. BOX 13819 MILWAUKEE, WI 53213

Visit Hal Leonard Online at
www.halleonard.com

ABC

Words and Music by ALPHONSO MIZELL, FREDERICK PERREN,
DEKE RICHARDS and BERRY GORDY

G
Cmaj7
G
4
4
I'm gon - na teach you all a - bout
Teach - er's gon - na show you how to get an
C
G
C
5
2
love, dear. Sit your - self down; take a seat;
"A"? Spell me you add the two,
G
C
all you got - ta do is re - peat af - ter me.
lis - ten to me ba - by, that's all you got - ta do.
G
Cmaj7
G
A B C eas - y as 1 2 3

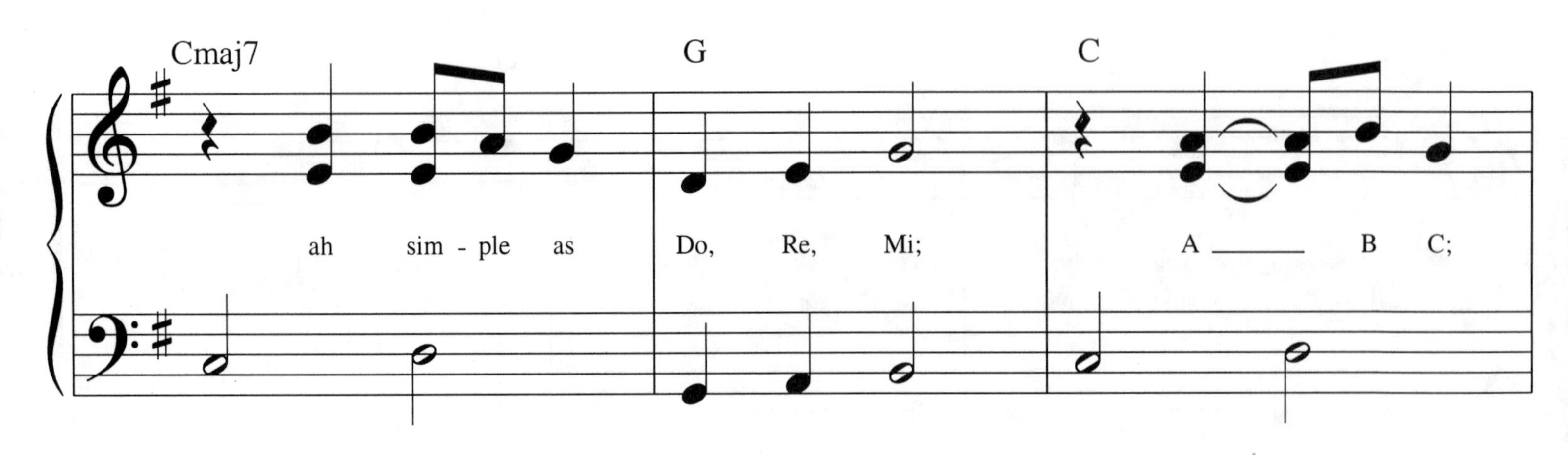
Cmaj7
G
C
ah sim - ple as
Do, Re, Mi;
A B C;

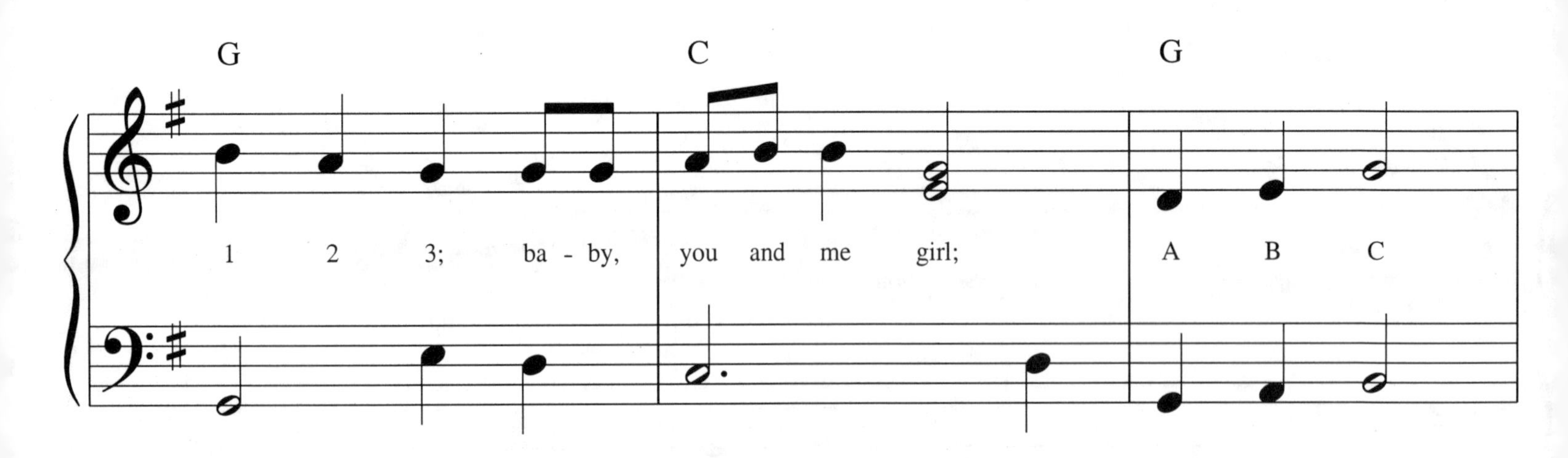
G
C
G
1 2 3; ba - by,
you and me girl;
A B C

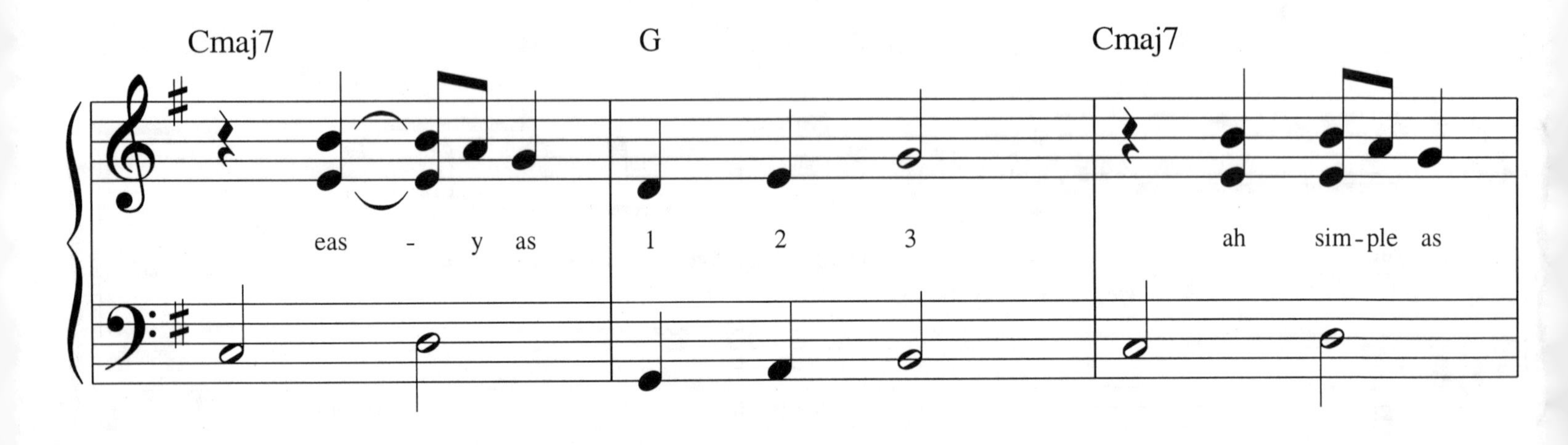
Cmaj7
G
Cmaj7
eas - y as
1 2 3
ah sim-ple as

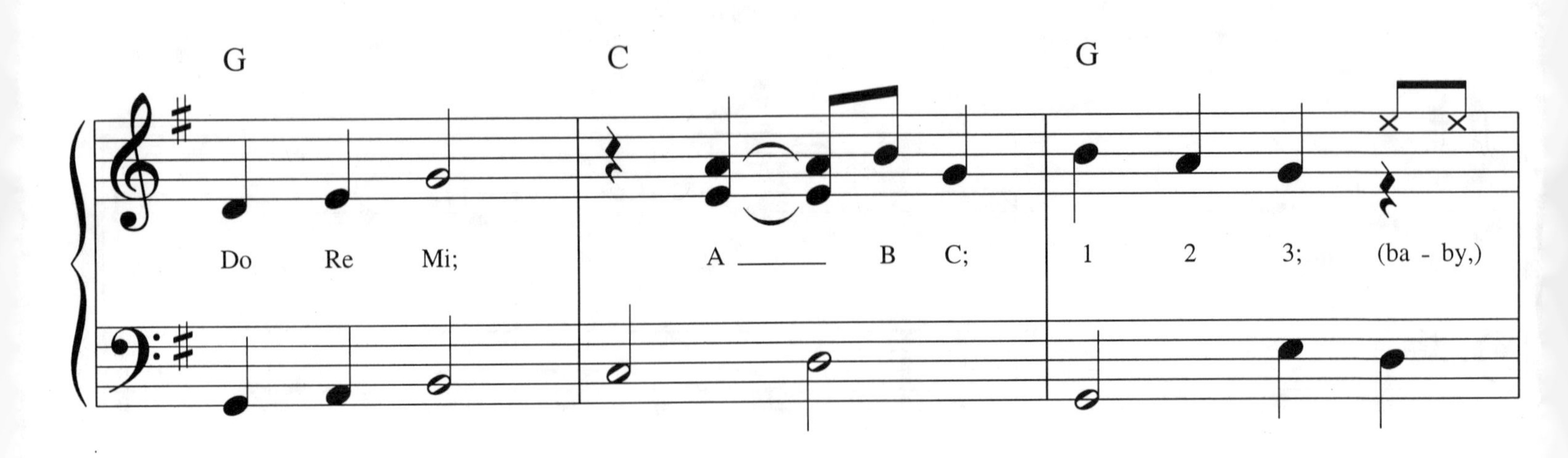
G
C
G
Do Re Mi;
A B C;
1 2 3; (ba - by,)

1.
C
G
you and me girl.
C
G
4
C
Come on, let me love you just a lit - tle bit;
G
3
C/G
G
1
I'm gon - na teach you how to sing it out.
Com - a, com - a, come on let me
C
2.
N.C.
show you what it's all a - bout.

Yah
sit down
girl
I think I
love you.
No
get up girl
show me what
you can do.
G
C/G
3
Shake it, shake it,
ba - by, come on now

G
C/G
G
shake it, shake it, ba - by. Oo, ___ shake it, shake it,
C
G
Cmaj7
ba - by, hey.
G
Cmaj7
G
gradually softer
C
G
C
G
5
1
5
1
mp
rit.

BEN

Words by DON BLACK
Music by WALTER SCHARF

F Bb F Bb Fm
me. Ben you're al-ways run-ning
C7/E Fm C7/E
here and there. You feel you're not want-ed an-y-where.
F A7
If you ev-er look be-hind and don't like what you
Eb7 D7 Db7 C7 F Bb
find, there's some-thing you should know. You've got a place to go.

F
B♭
Gm7
C7
F
I used to say
I and me.
1
2
Gm7
C7
F
2
Gm7
C7
Now it's us,
now it's we.
I
used to say
F
Gm7
C7
F
I and me.
Now it's us,
now it's we.
C7/E
F
Ben, most peo - ple would turn
you a - way.
I don't lis - ten to a

C7/E
F
4
C7/E
word they say.
They don't see you as I
do; I wish they would try
5
E♭7
D7
D♭7♯5
C7
3
to. I'm sure they'd think a - gain if they had a friend like
1

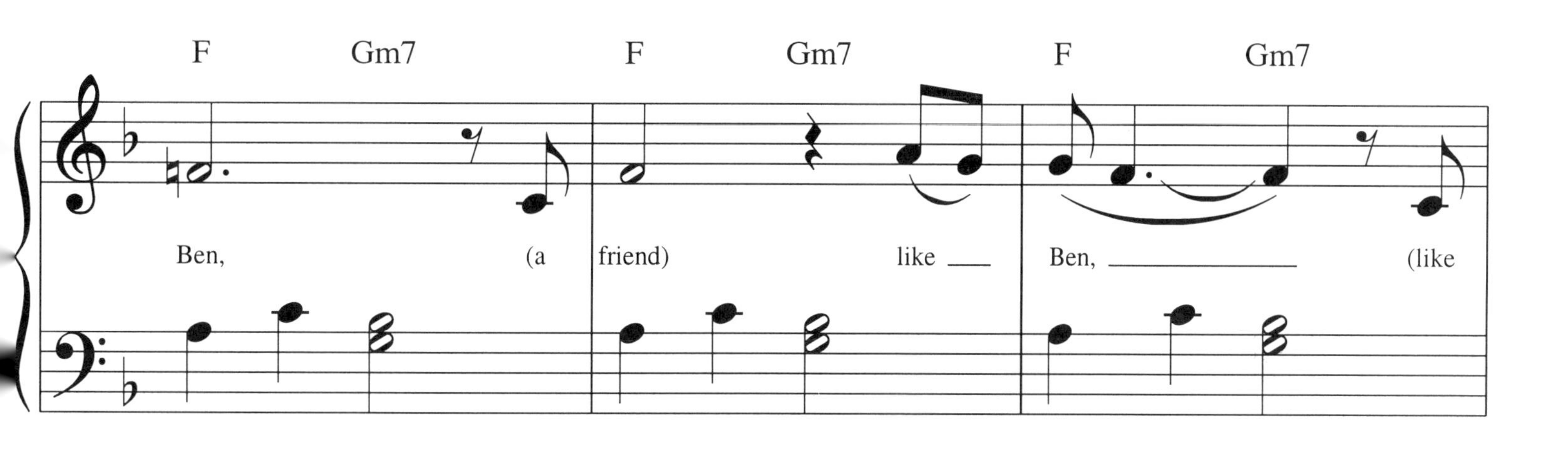
F
Gm7
F
Gm7
F
Gm7
Ben, (a friend) like Ben, (like

F
Gm7
F
Ben,) like Ben.
rit.

I CAN'T HELP MYSELF
(SUGAR PIE, HONEY BUNCH)

Words and Music by BRIAN HOLLAND,
LAMONT DOZIER and EDWARD HOLLAND

Em
F
G
5
I love ___ you and
no - bod - y else. ___
I'm a _____ fool in
love you see. ___
Wan - na
C
In and out my life
you come and you
tell you I don't love you,
tell you that we're through, and I've
G
Dm
2
go,
leav - ing just your
pic - ture be - hind __________
tried.
But ev - 'ry time I
see your face __________
Em
F
G
To Coda
4
and I kissed it a
thou - sand times. _
I get all ___ choked
up ____ in - side. __

C
G
When you snap your fin - ger or wink your eye I come a - run - ning to you.

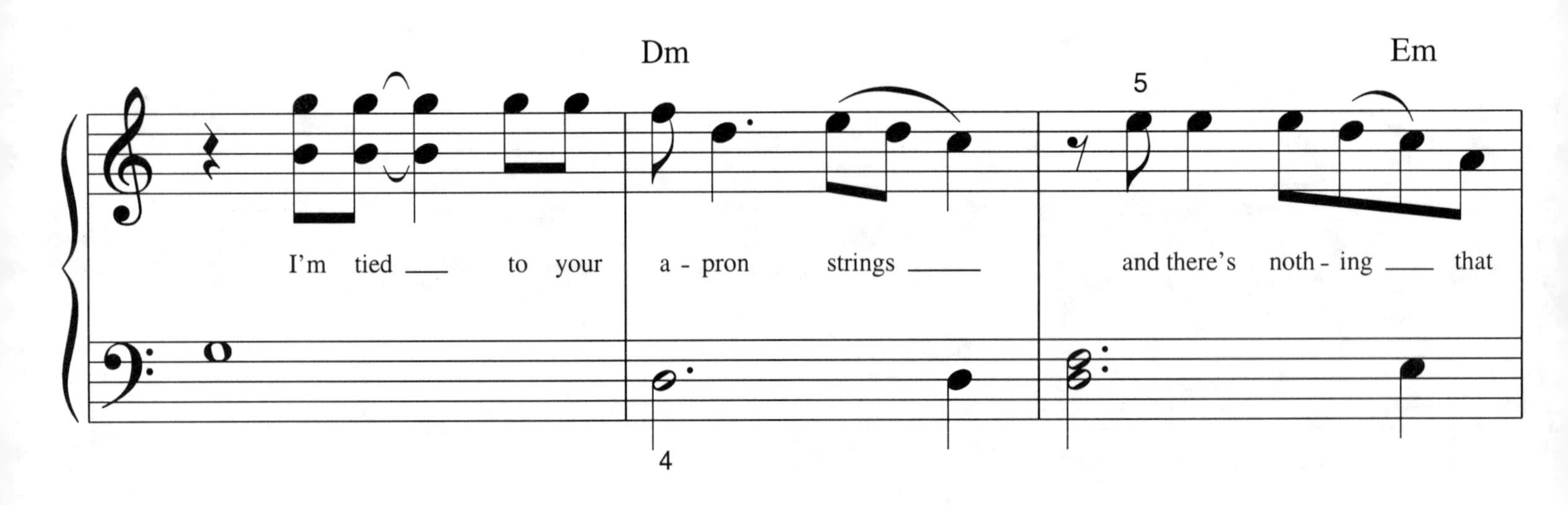
Dm
Em
5
I'm tied to your a - pron strings and there's noth - ing that
4

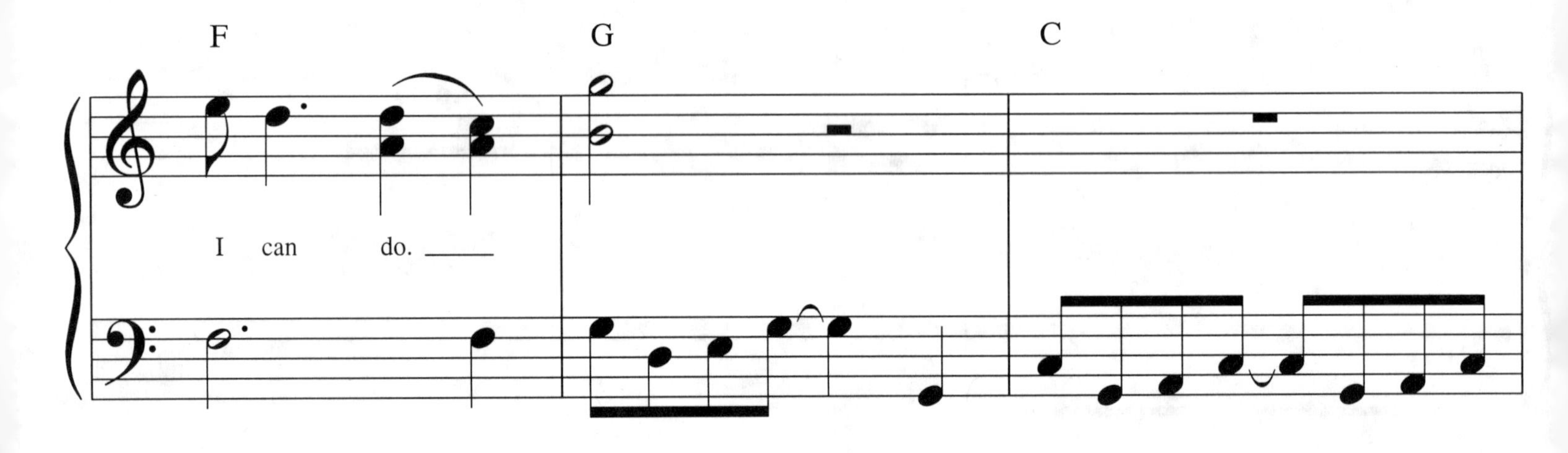
F
G
C
I can do.

N.C.
G
Can't

Dm
Em F
help my - self,
no I can't
help my - self.
G
D.S. al Coda
CODA
C
When I call your name,
girl, it starts the flame
burn-ing in my heart,
tear-ing it all a - part. No
mat - ter how I try, my
love I can - not hide. 'Cause
C
sug - ar - pie, hon - ey bunch,
sug - ar - pie, hon - ey bunch,

G
you know that I'm weak for you. Can't
do an - y - thing you ask me to. Can't
Dm
Em
F
5
help my - self, I love you and no - bod - y else.
help my - self, I want you and no - bod - y else.
1.
2.
G
G
N.C.
C

I HEAR A SYMPHONY

Words and Music by Edward Holland,
Lamont Dozier and Brian Holland

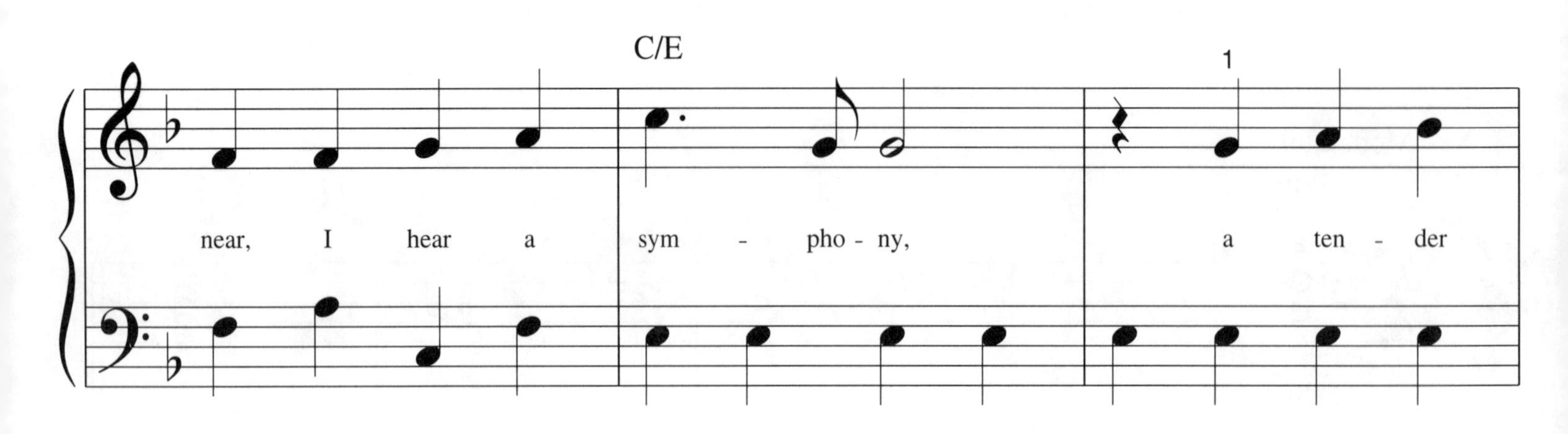
C/E
1
near, I hear a sym - pho - ny, a ten - der

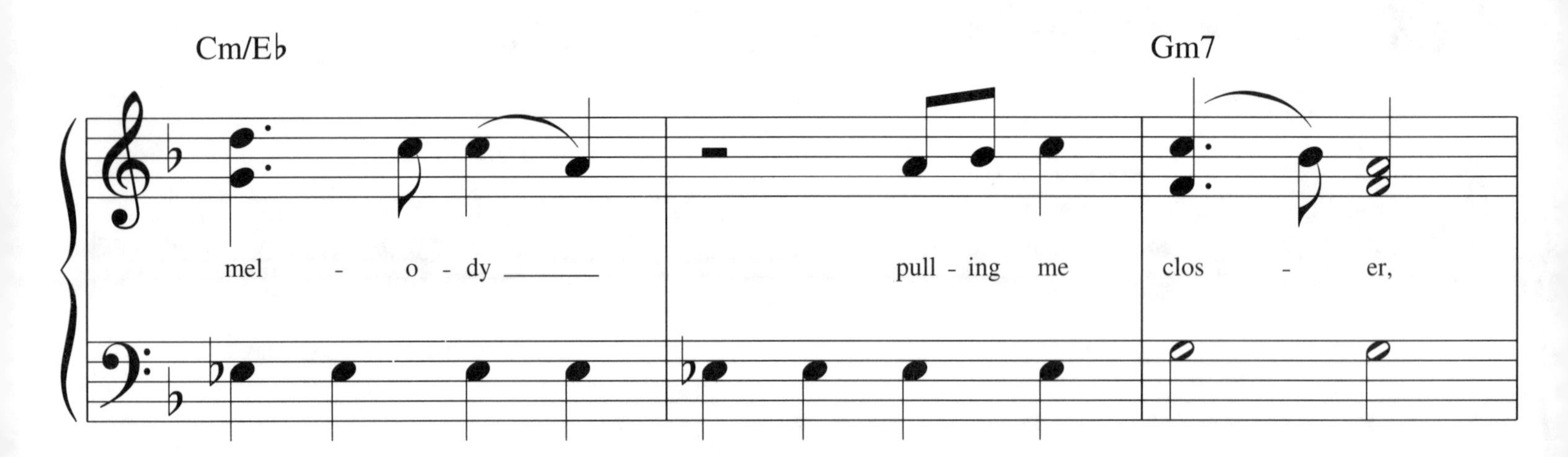
Cm/E♭
Gm7
mel - o - dy pull - ing me clos - er,

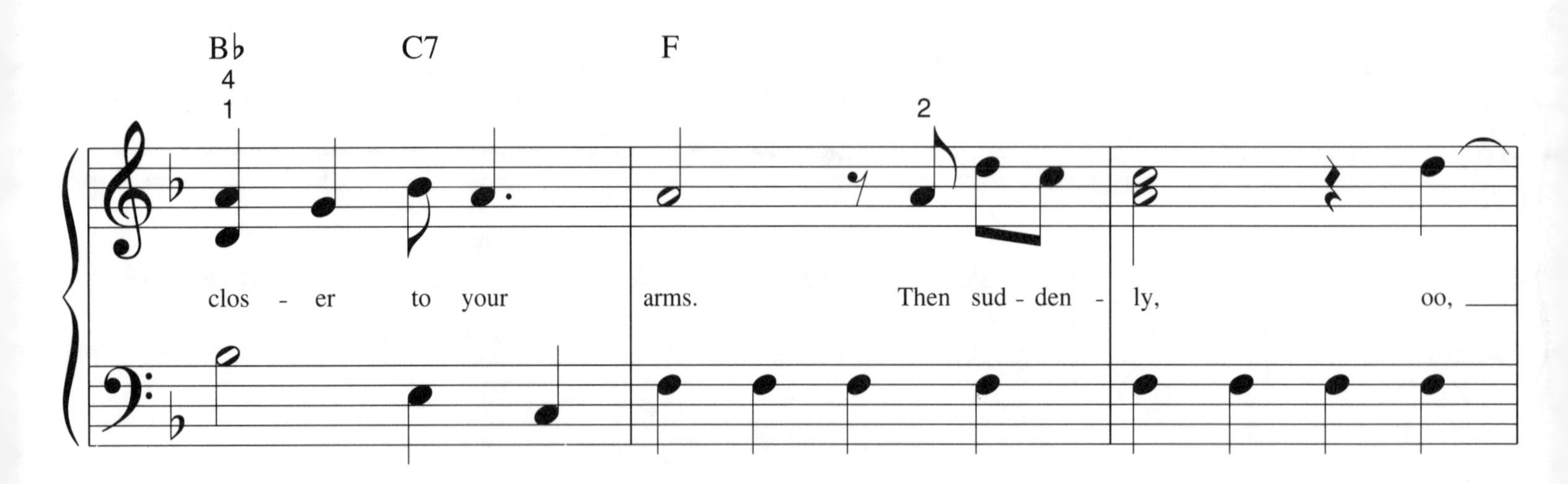
B♭
C7
F
4
1
2
clos - er to your arms. Then sud - den - ly, oo,

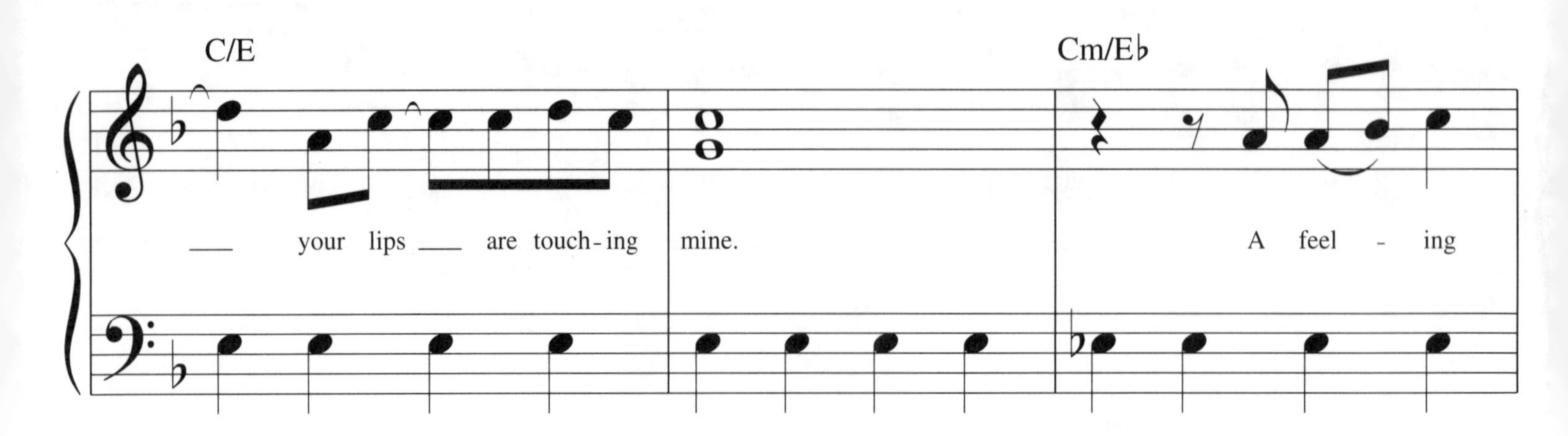
C/E
Cm/E♭
your lips are touch - ing mine. A feel - ing

Gm7
B♭
C7
so di - vine 'til I leave the past be - hind.
B♭m
A♭
I'm lost in a world made for you and
Fm
Gm7
F
D
me. Oo, love me. When - ev - er you are
G
D/F♯
near I hear a sym - pho - ny

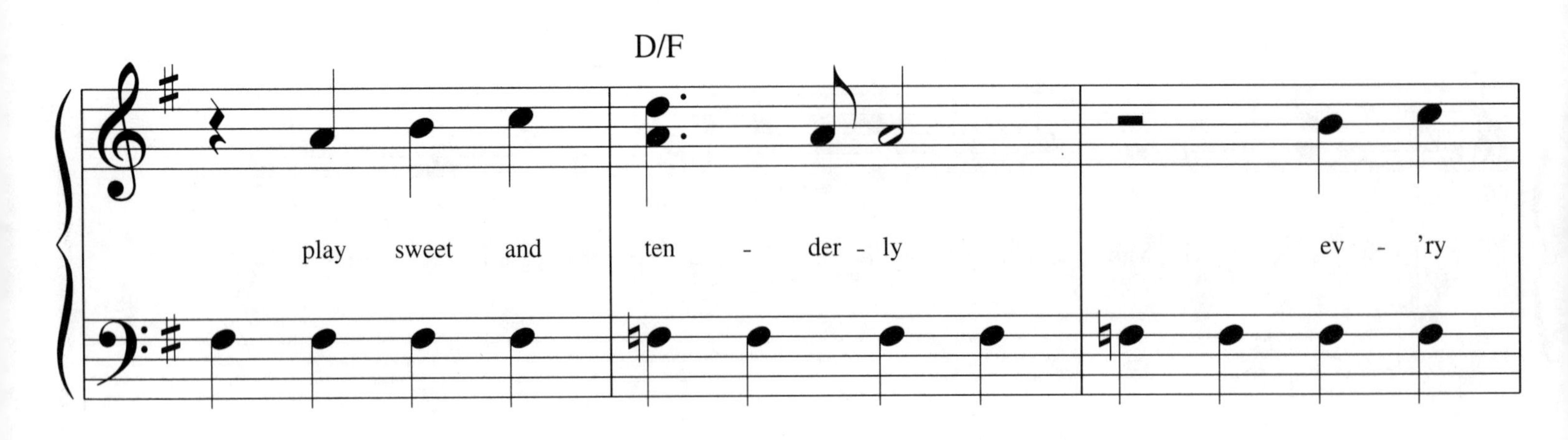
D/F
play sweet and ten - der - ly ev - 'ry

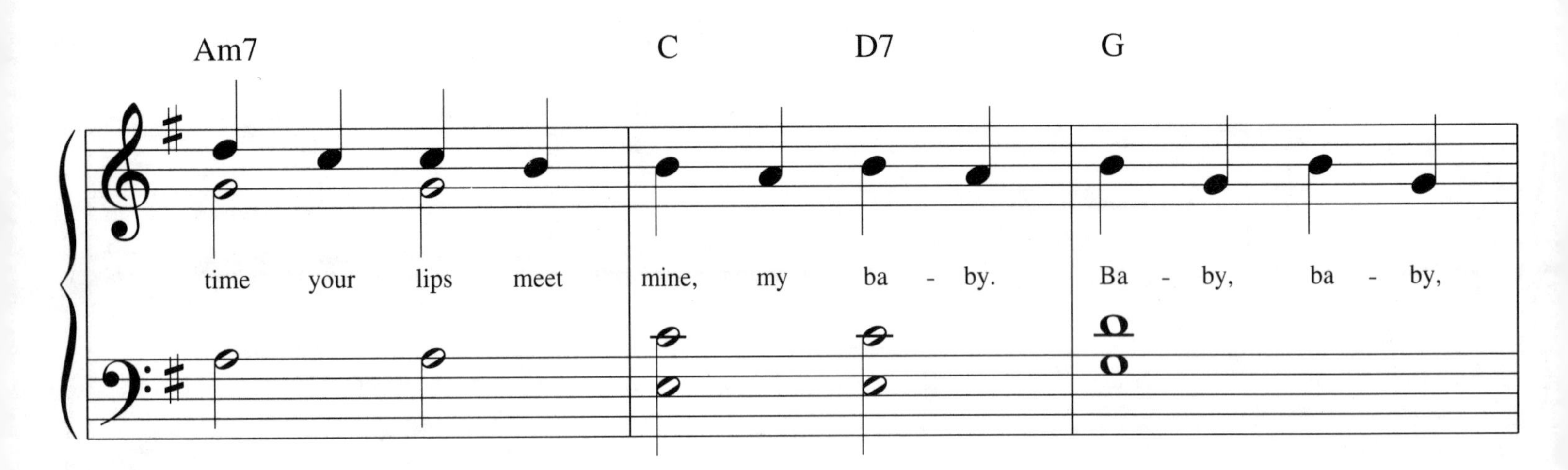
Am7
C
D7
G
time your lips meet mine, my ba - by. Ba - by, ba - by,

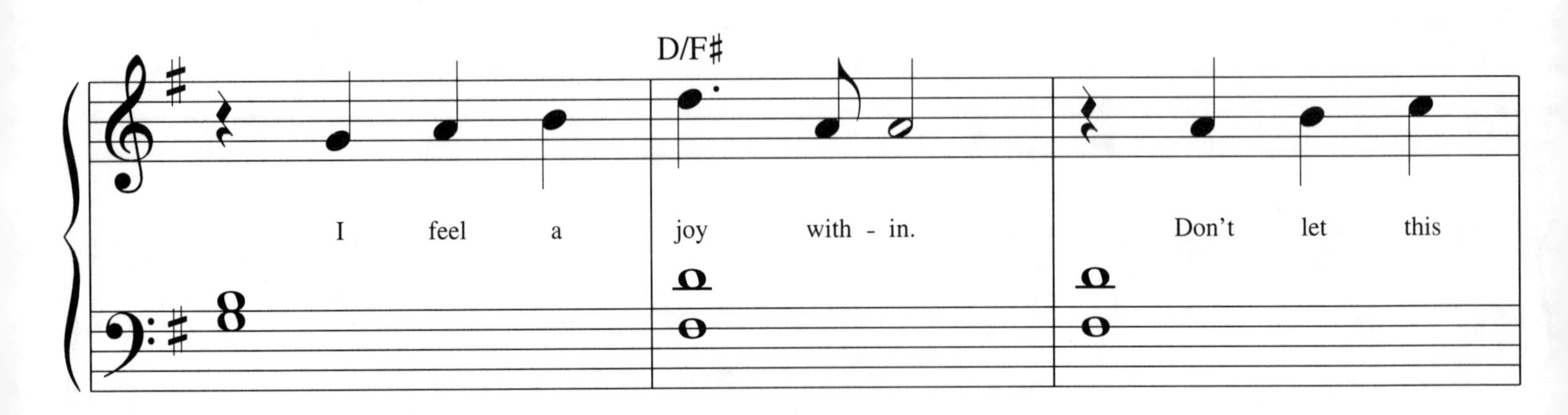
D/F#
I feel a joy with - in. Don't let this
8

Dm/F
Am7
C
G7
feel - ing end; let it go on and on and on now, ba - by.

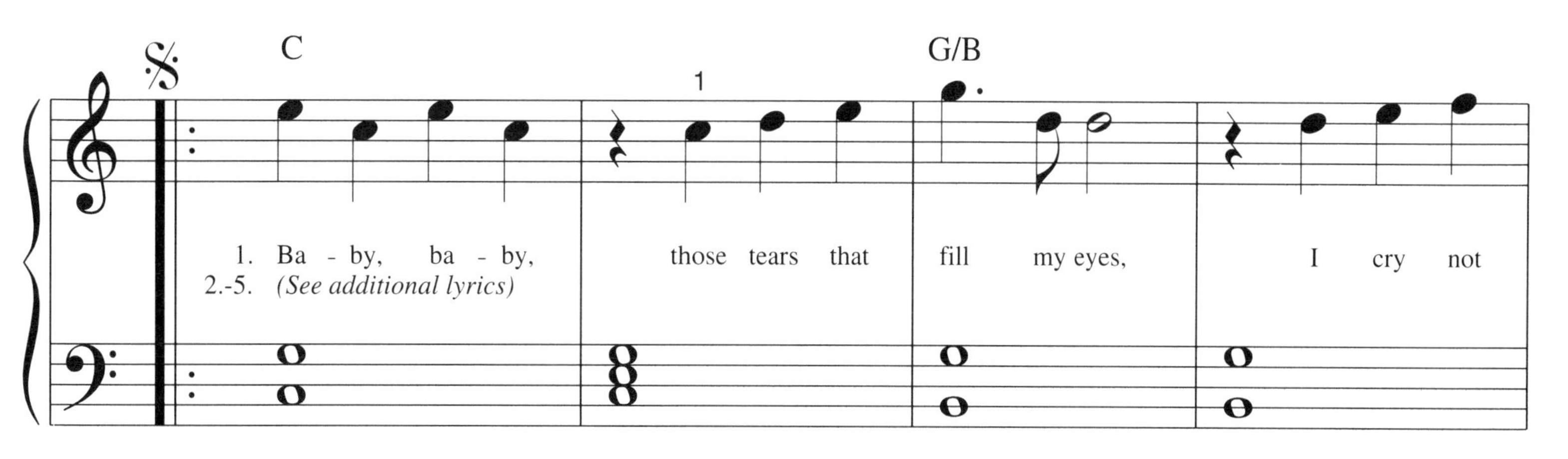

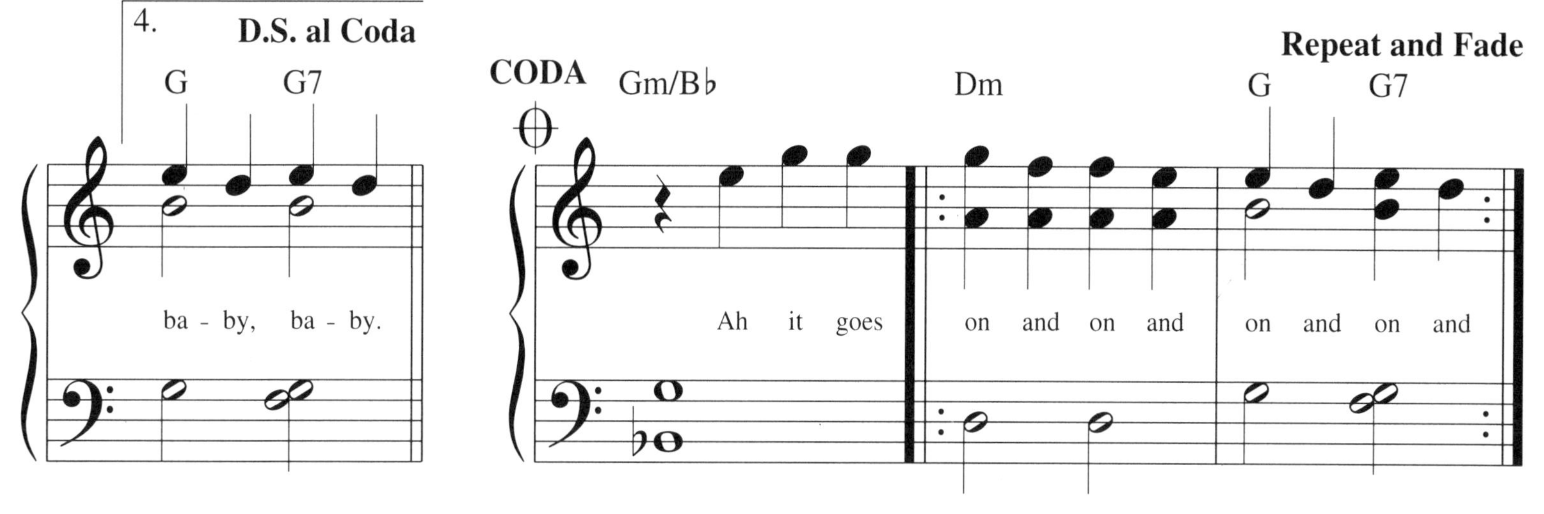

Additional Lyrics

2. Whenever you are near, I hear a symphony.
   Each time you speak to me I hear a tender rhapsody of love, love.

3. Baby, baby as you stand up holding me
   Whispering how much you care,
   A thousand violins fill the air now.

4. Baby, baby, don't let this moment end,
   Keep standing close to me,
   Oo, so close to me, baby, baby.

5. Baby, baby, I hear a symphony,
   A tender melody,
   Ah, it goes on and on and on and on and.....

I HEARD IT THROUGH THE GRAPEVINE

Words and Music by
Norman J. Whitfield and Barrett Strong

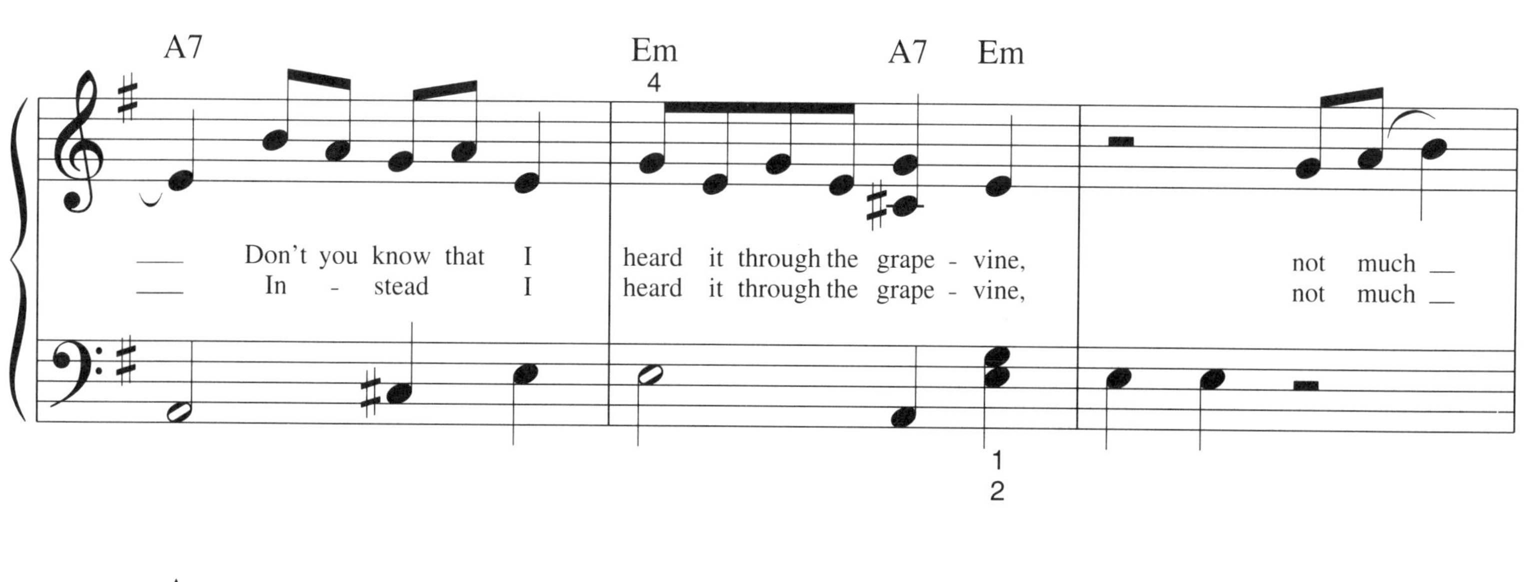
A7
Em
A7
Em
Don't you know that I heard it through the grape - vine, not much
In - stead I heard it through the grape - vine, not much

A
Em
A7
Em
long - er would you be mine. Uh huh, heard it through the grape - vine.
long - er would you be mine. Oh, I heard it through the grape - vine,

A7
Oh, I'm just a - bout to lose my mind.
and I'm just a - bout to lose my mind.
Hon - ey, hon - ey, oh
(I

Em
To Coda
yeah.
heard it through the grape-vine, not much long - er would you be mine, ba - by.)

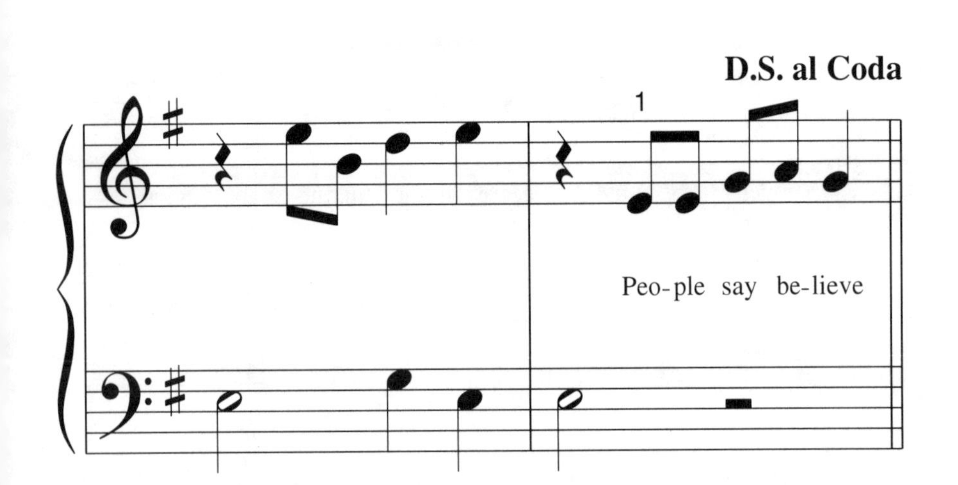

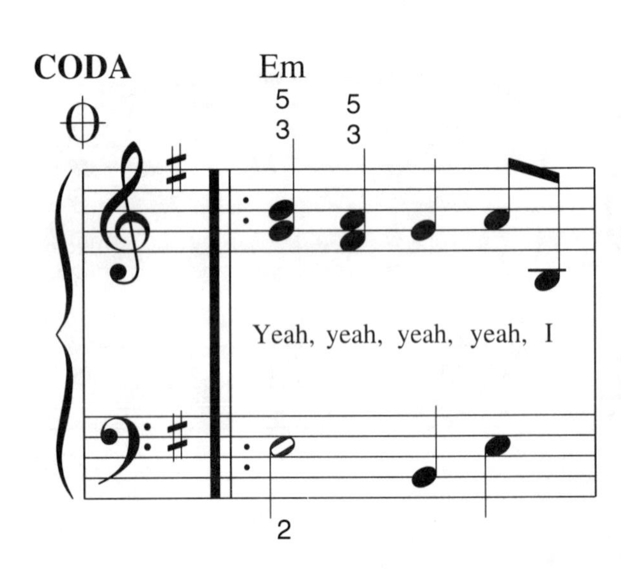

Additional Lyrics

3. People say believe half of what you see
   Oh, and none of what you hear;
   But I can't help but be confused
   If it's true, please tell me dear.
   Do you plan to let me go
   For the other guy you loved before?

I'LL BE THERE

Words and Music by Berry Gordy, Hal Davis,
Willie Hutch and Bob West

C/E
Dm
Dm/C
Am
hand to you, I'll have faith in all you do.
tect you with an un - self - ish love that re - spects you.

B♭
Gm7
B♭/C
F
Just call my name, and I'll be there.

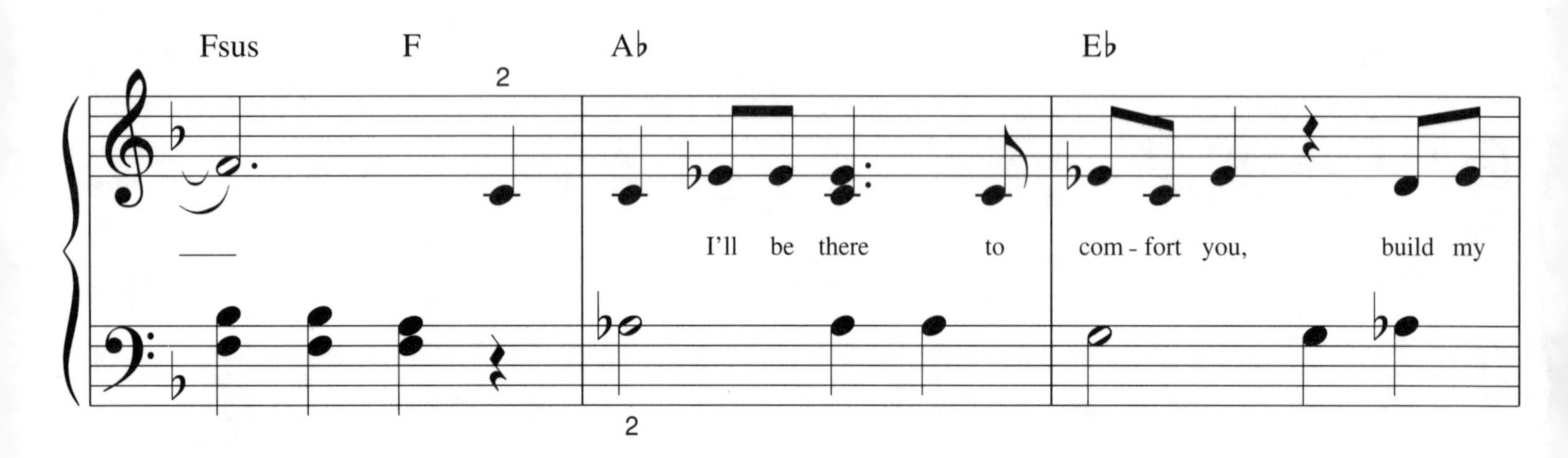

Fsus
F
A♭
E♭
I'll be there to com - fort you, build my

B♭
F
A♭
world of dreams a - round you. I'm so glad I found you. I'll be there with a love

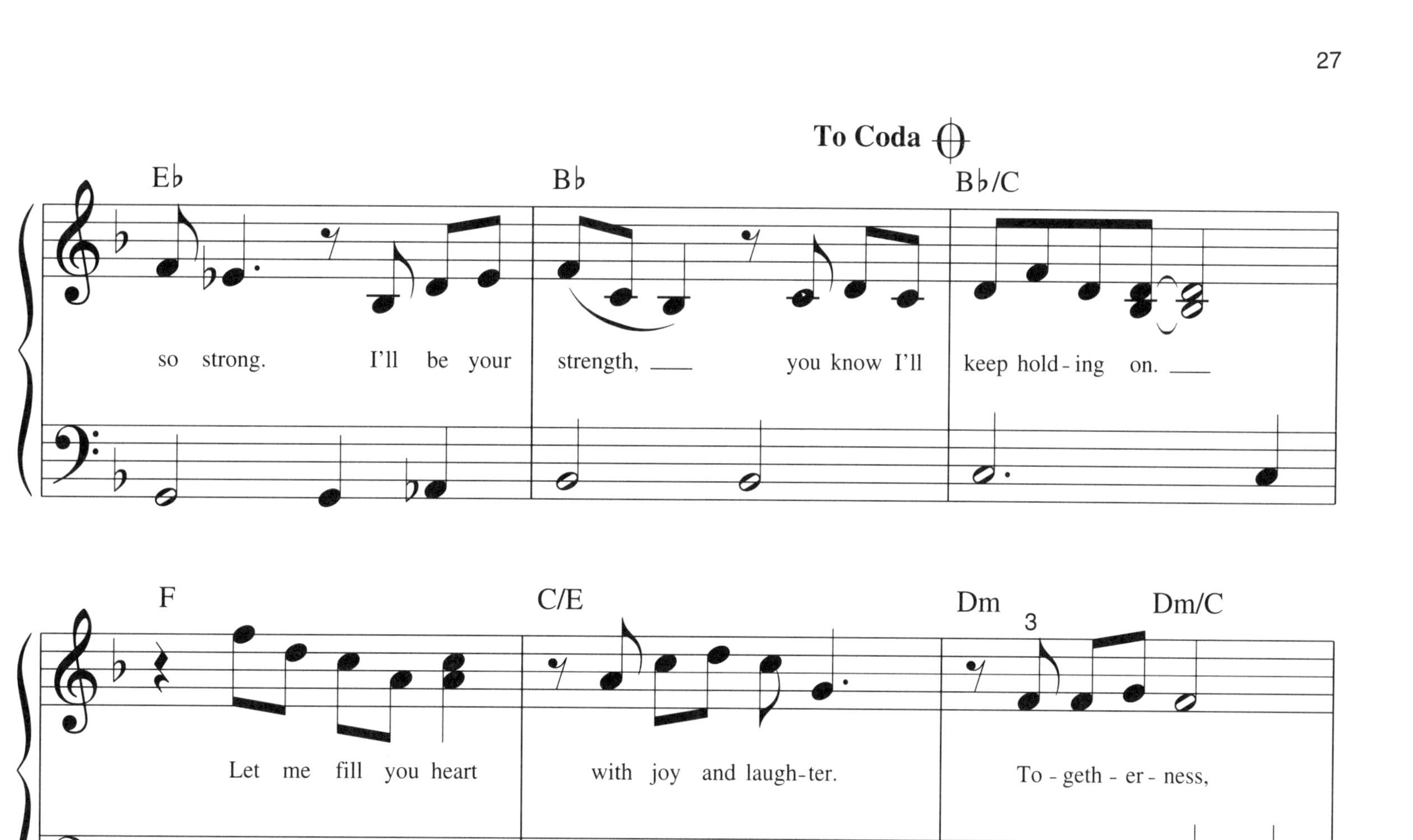
To Coda
E♭
B♭
B♭/C
so strong. I'll be your
strength, ___ you know I'll
keep hold - ing on. ___
F
C/E
Dm
Dm/C
3
Let me fill you heart
with joy and laugh-ter.
To - geth - er - ness,
1

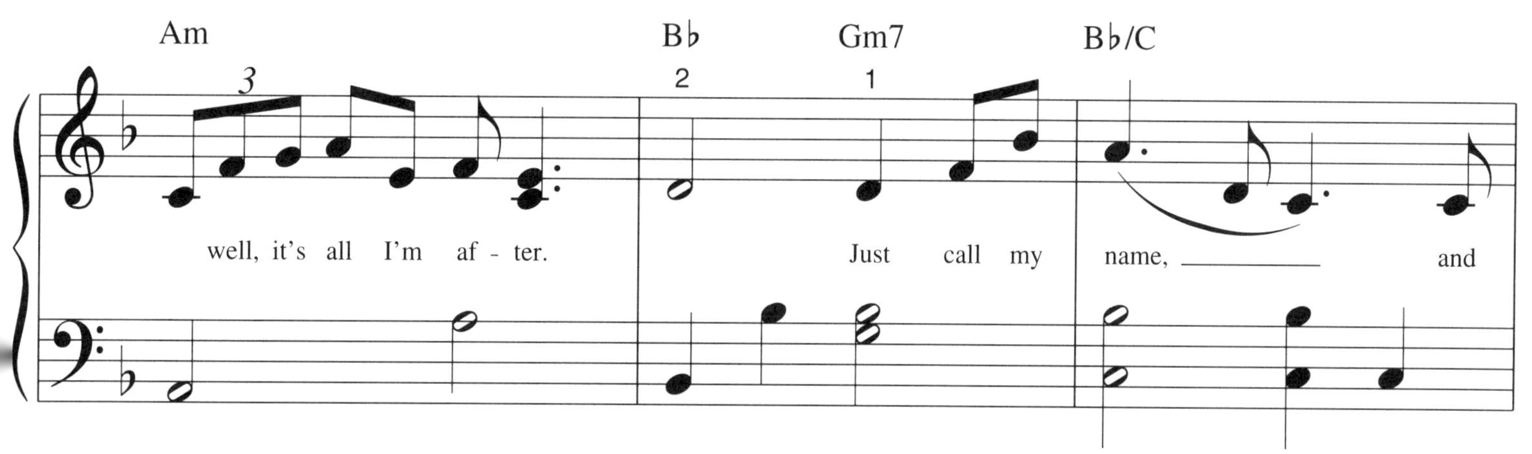
Am
B♭
Gm7
B♭/C
3
2
1
well, it's all I'm af - ter.
Just call my
name, ___ and

F
C7sus
D.S. al Coda
I'll be there. ___

CODA
B♭/C
keep hold-ing on. ___

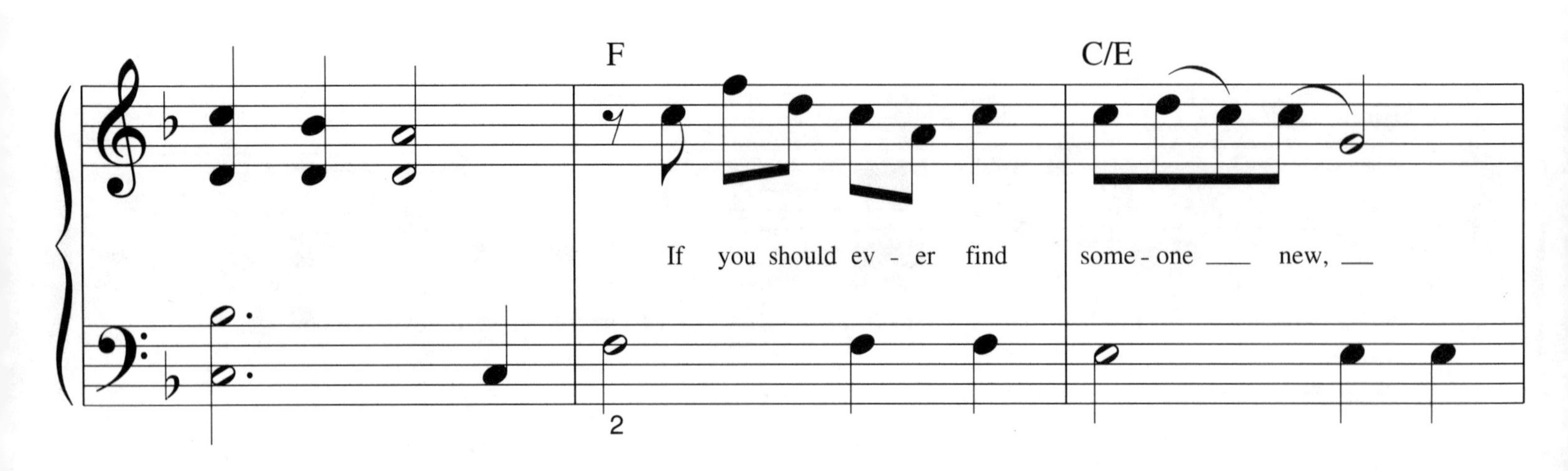
F
C/E
If you should ever find someone new,

Dm
Dm/C
Am
B♭
Gm7
I know she'd bet - ter be good to you.
'cause if she

B♭/C
F
C7sus
does - n't, then I'll be there.
Don't you know, ba - by,

F
C/E
Dm
Dm/C
I'll be there,
I'll be

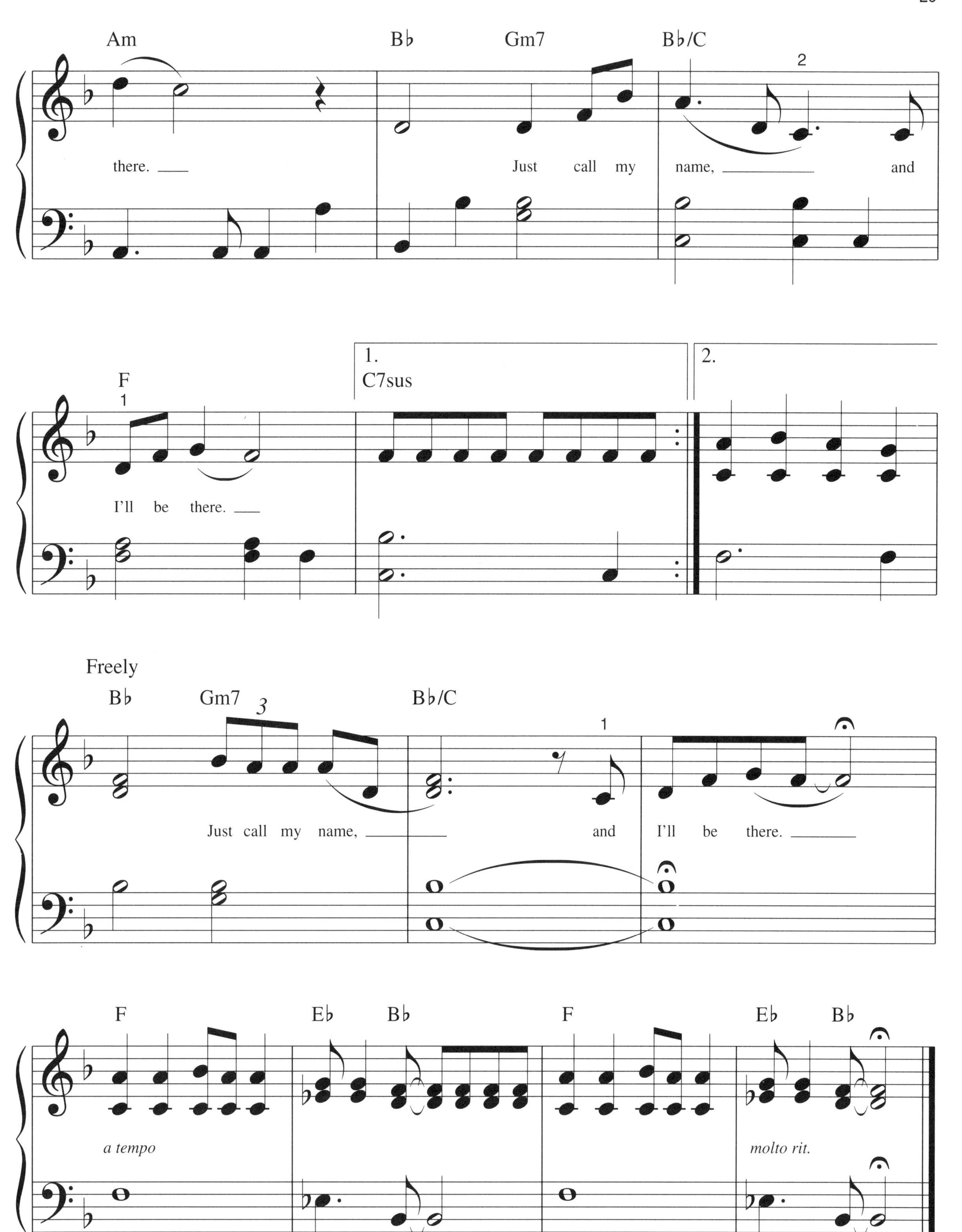
Am
B♭
Gm7
B♭/C
there.
Just call my
name,
and
F
1.
C7sus
2.
I'll be there.
Freely
B♭
Gm7
B♭/C
Just call my name,
and
I'll be there.
F
E♭
B♭
F
E♭
B♭
a tempo
molto rit.

JUST MY IMAGINATION (RUNNING AWAY WITH ME)

Words and Music by
Norman J. Whitfield and Barrett Strong

Dm7
G7
C
Out of all the fel - lows in the
this couldn't be a dream for too
world, she be - longs to me.
real it all seems.
But it was
G7sus
just my i-mag - i - na - tion,
(once a - gain)
Run-nin' a - way with me.
It was
(Tell you it was)
just my i - mag - i - na - tion run-nin' a -
To Coda

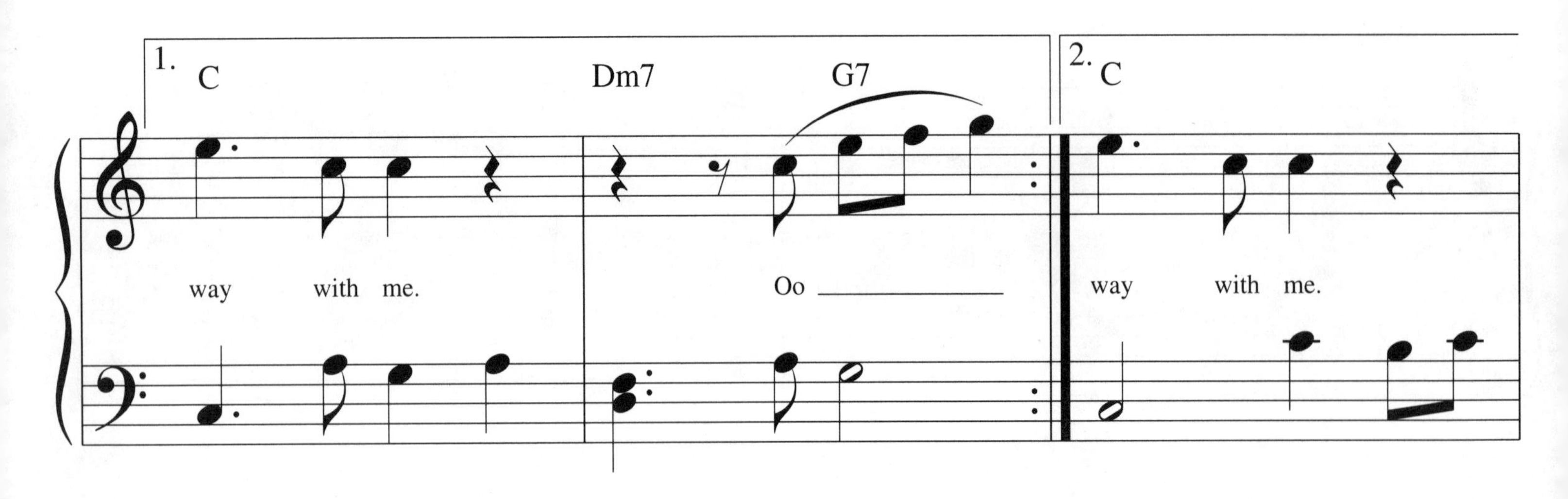
1.
C
Dm7
G7
2.
C
way with me.
Oo
way with me.

Ev - 'ry night on my

knees I pray:
Dear Lord,
hear my plea,

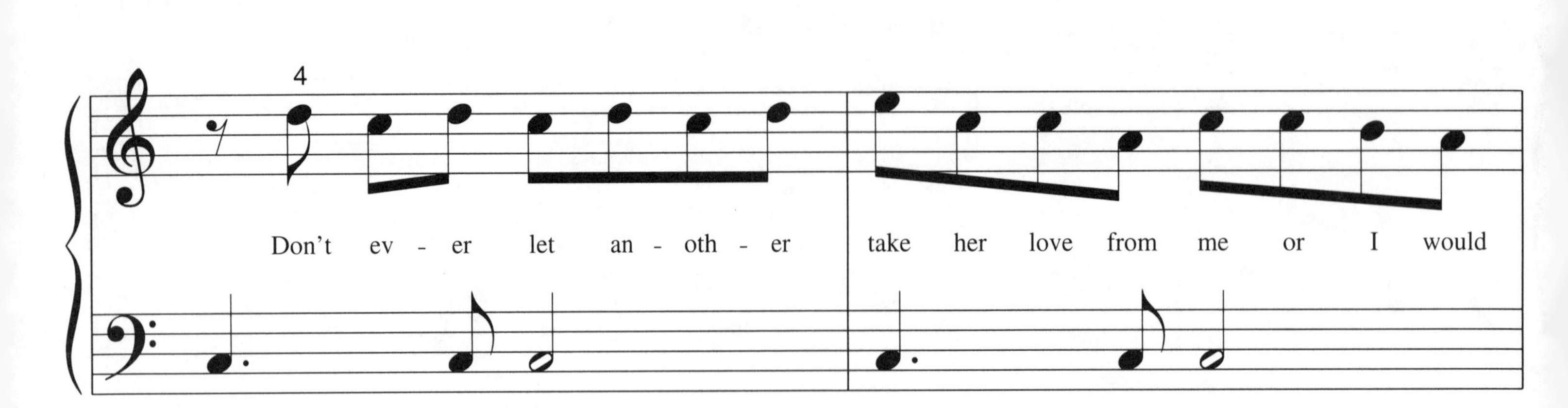
Don't ev - er let an - oth - er
take her love from me or I would

G7
C
sure - ly die.
Her love is
heav - en - ly.

When her arms en - fold me,
I hear a ten - der rhap - so -

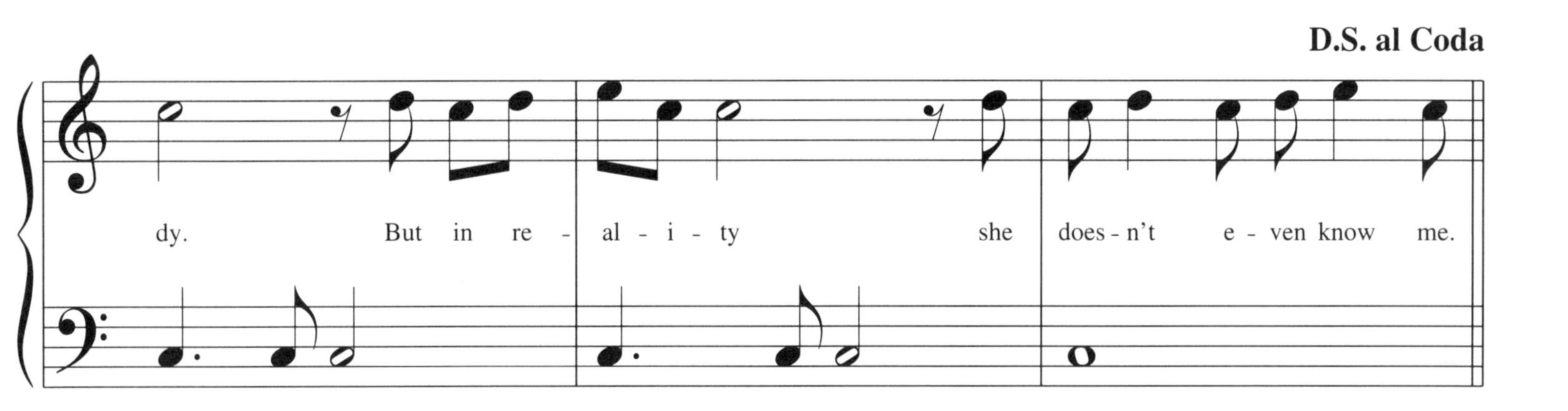
D.S. al Coda
dy. But in re -
al - i - ty she
does - n't e - ven know me.

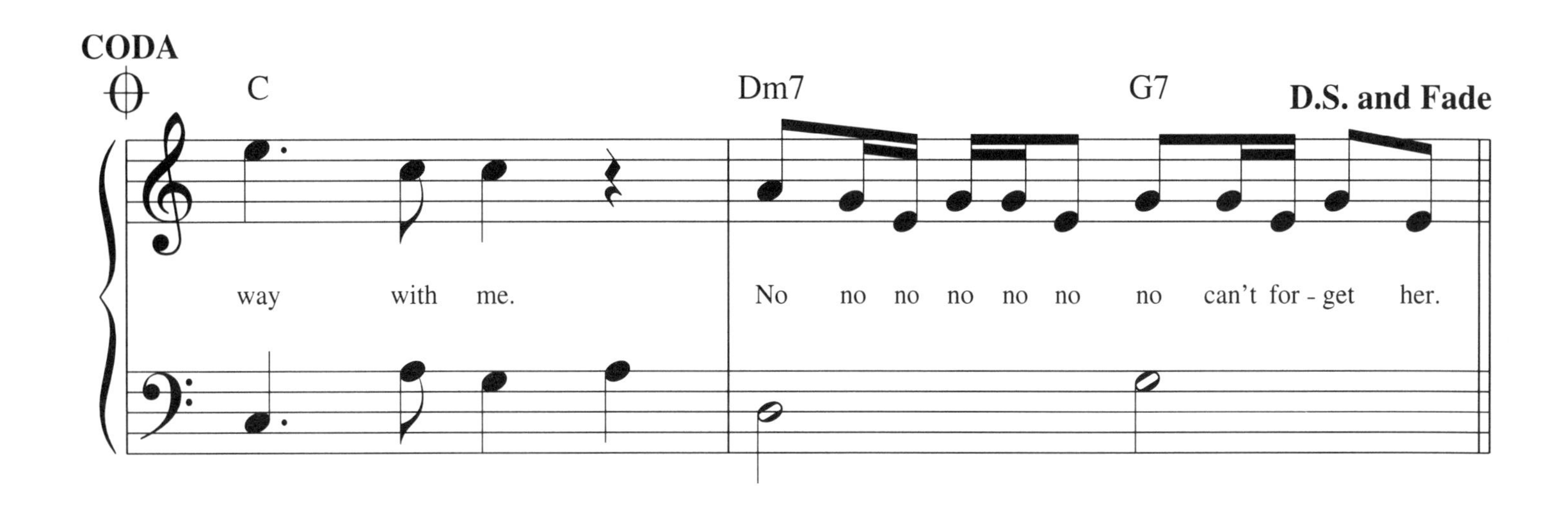
CODA
C
Dm7
G7
D.S. and Fade
way with me.
No no no no no no no can't for - get her.

MY CHERIE AMOUR

Words and Music by STEVIE WONDER,
SYLVIA MOY and HENRY COSBY

Fmaj7
D7
Gmaj7
day,
street,
My Che - rie a - mour
I've been near you but you
C9
Fmaj7
D7
dis - tant as the Milk - y Way.
nev - er no - ticed me.
My Che -
My Che -
Cmaj7
D7
rie a - mour,
rie a - mour,
pret - ty lit - tle one that
won't you tell me how could
F7
E7
I a - dore,
you ig - nore,
You're the on - ly girl my
That be - hind that lit - tle

A7
D7
To Coda
heart beats for,
smile I wore,
How I wish that you were
How I wish that you were
3
5
1.
G
D7
2.
G
mine.
In a
mine.
1
2
D7
Cmaj7
Fmaj7
La la
la la la
la, La la
F7
Gmaj7
D.S. al Coda
CODA
G
la la la
la. May - be
mine.

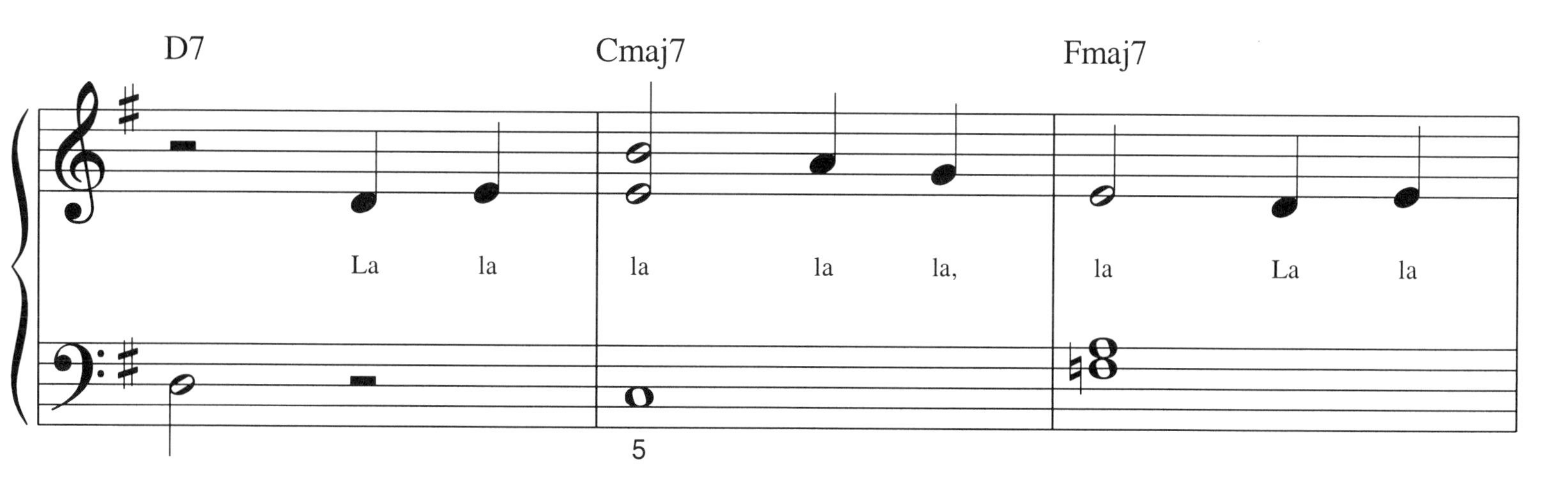

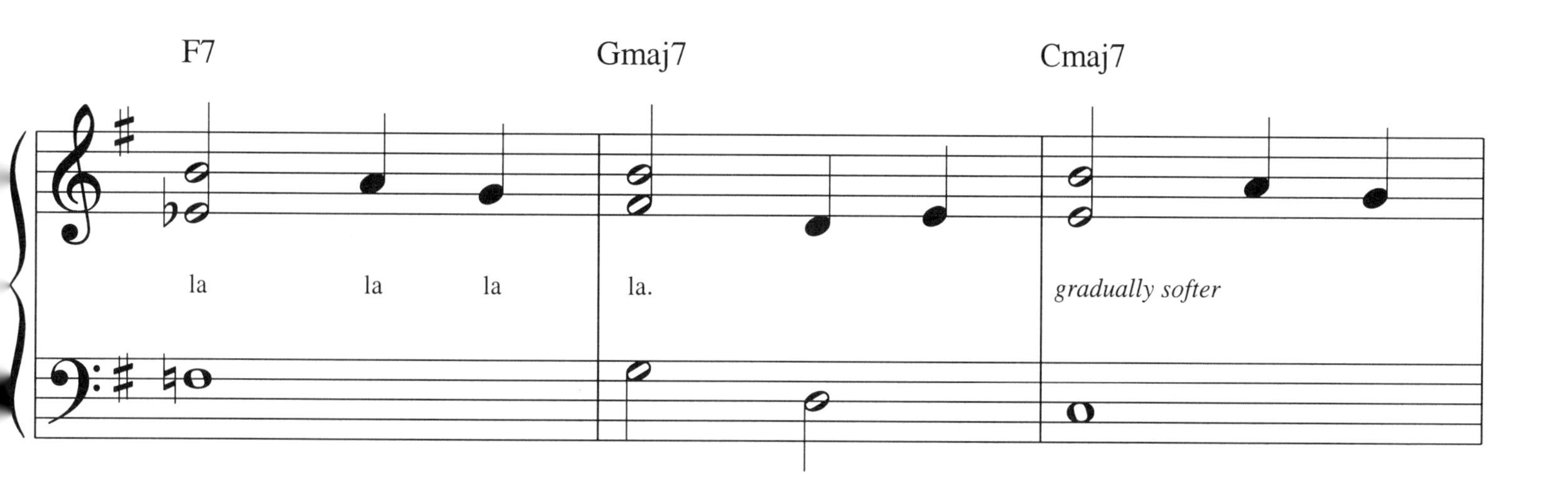

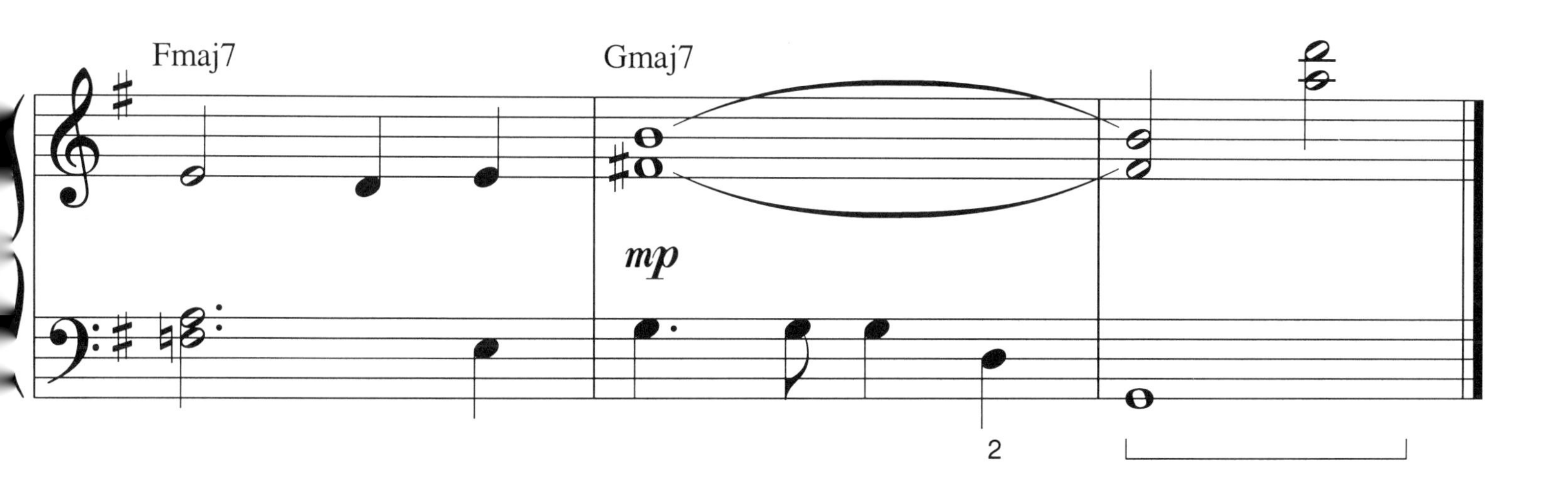

Additional Lyrics

3. Maybe someday you'll see my face among the crowd,
   Maybe someday I'll share your little distant cloud.
   Oh, Cherie amour, pretty little one that I adore,
   You're the only girl my heart beats for,
   How I wish that you were mine.

MY GIRL

Words and Music by
William "Smokey" Robinson and Ronald White

B♭ C F
feel this way? My girl, talk - ing 'bout

B♭ C7 F
my girl. I've got so much

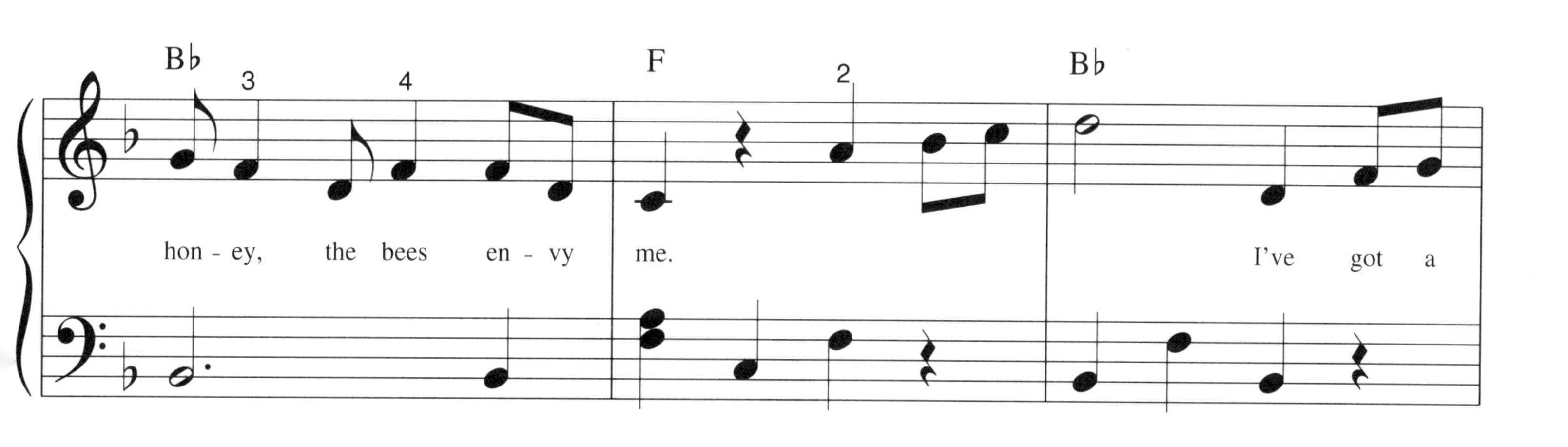
B♭ F B♭
hon - ey, the bees en - vy me. I've got a

F B♭ F
sweet - er song than the birds in the tree.

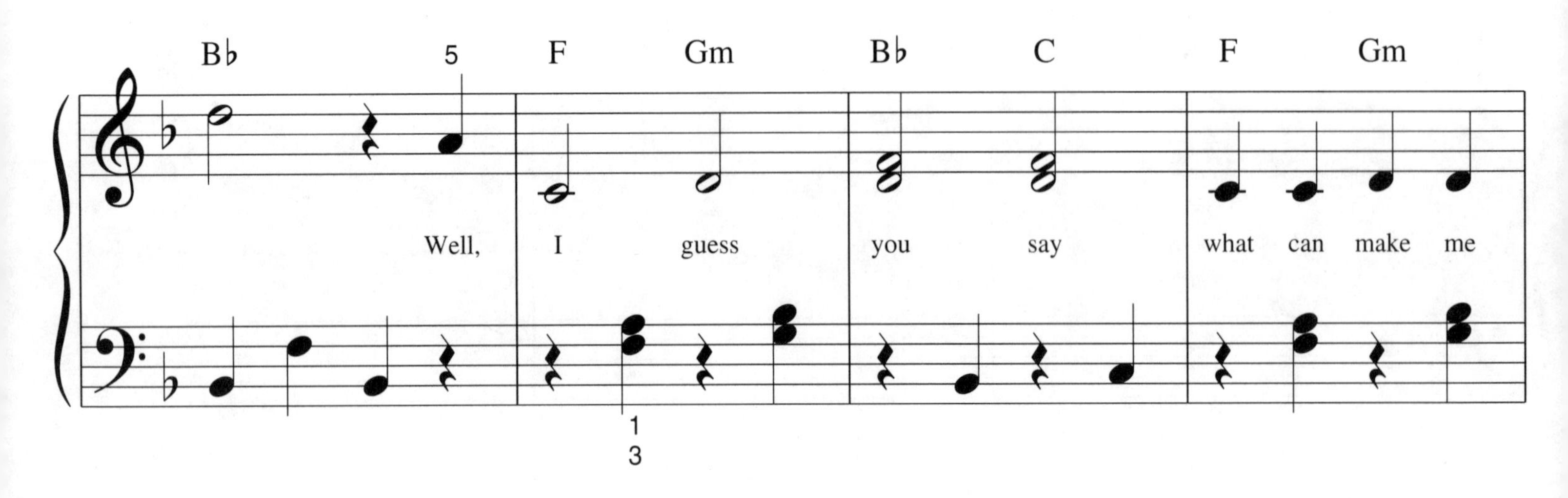
B♭
5
F
Gm
B♭
C
F
Gm
Well,
I
guess
you
say
what can make me
1
3

B♭
C
F
3
feel this way?
My girl,
talk - ing 'bout
1
2

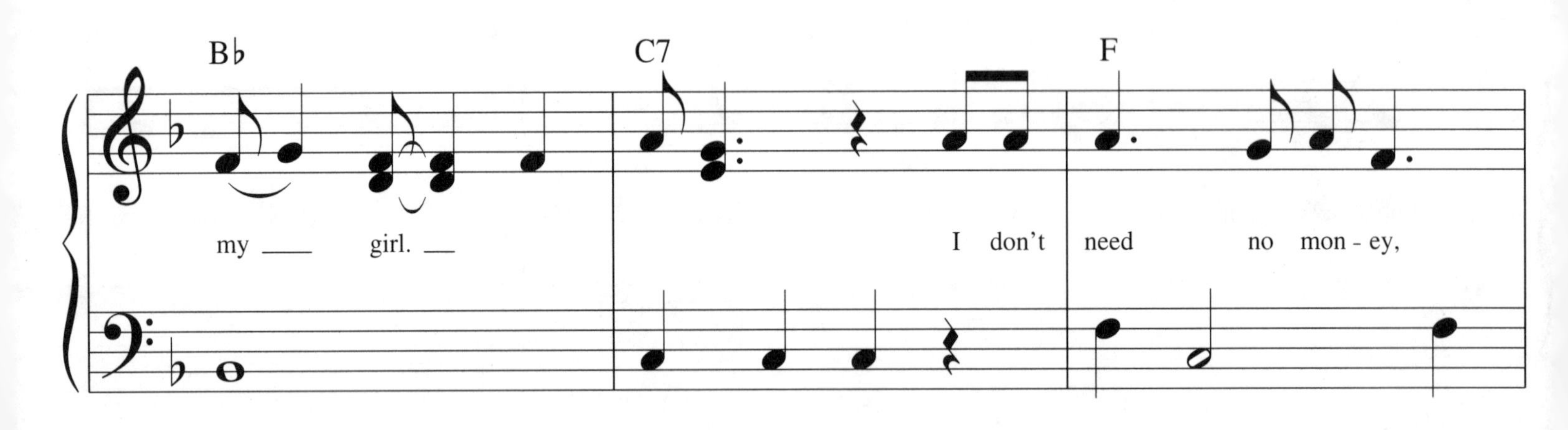
B♭
C7
F
my girl.
I don't
need
no mon - ey,

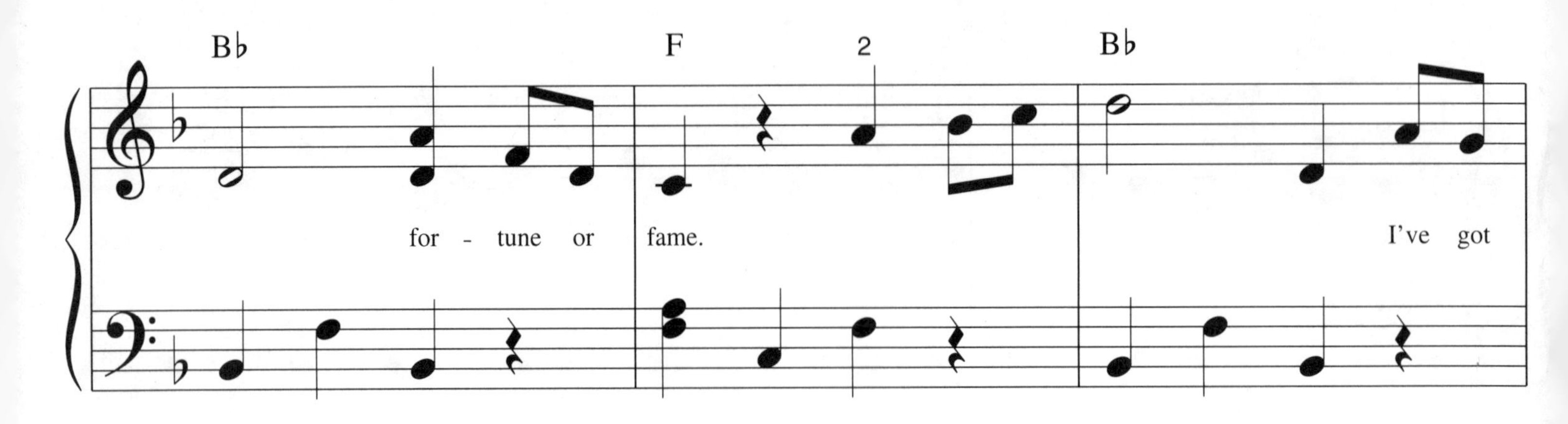
B♭
F
2
B♭
for - tune or
fame.
I've got

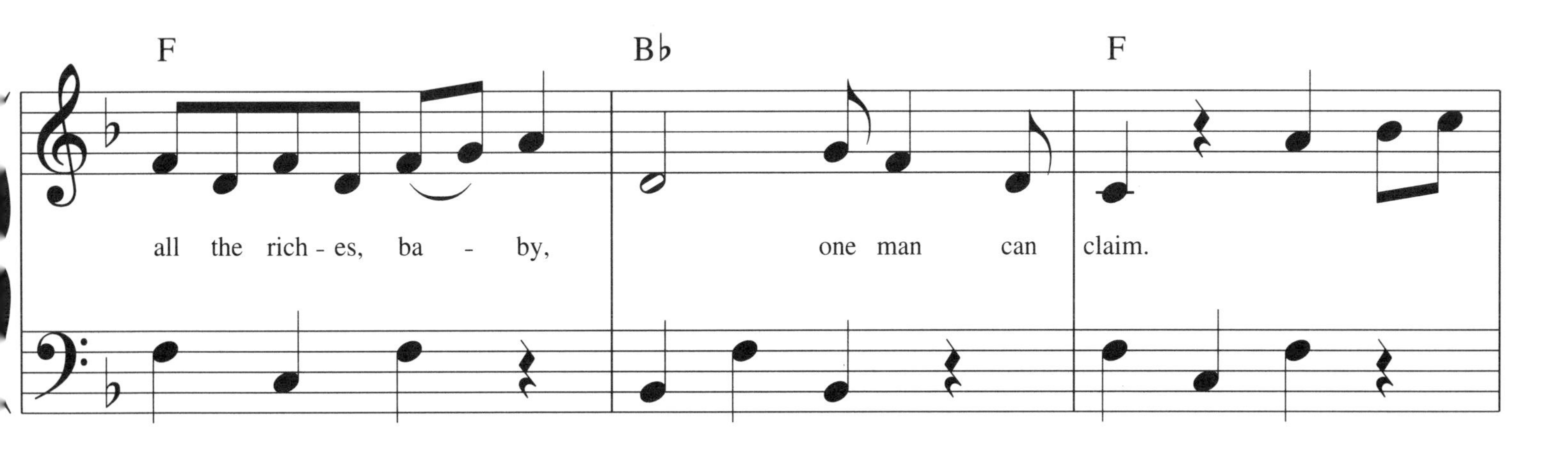
F
B♭
F
all the rich - es, ba - by,
one man can
claim.

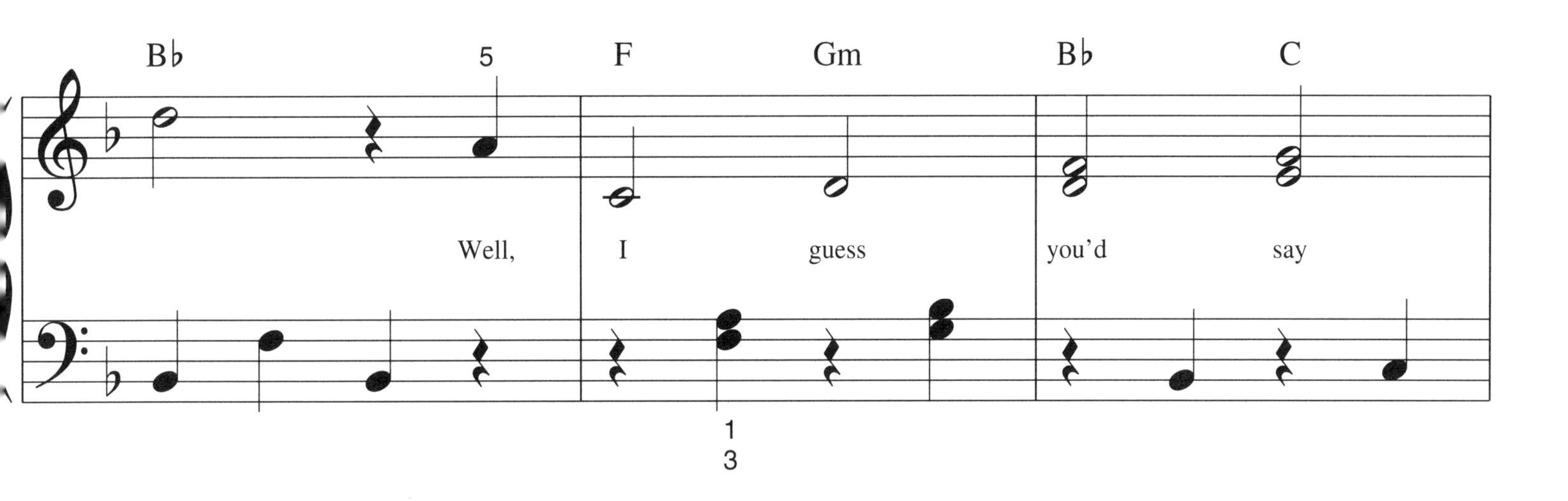
B♭
5
F
Gm
B♭
C
Well,
I
guess
you'd
say
1
3

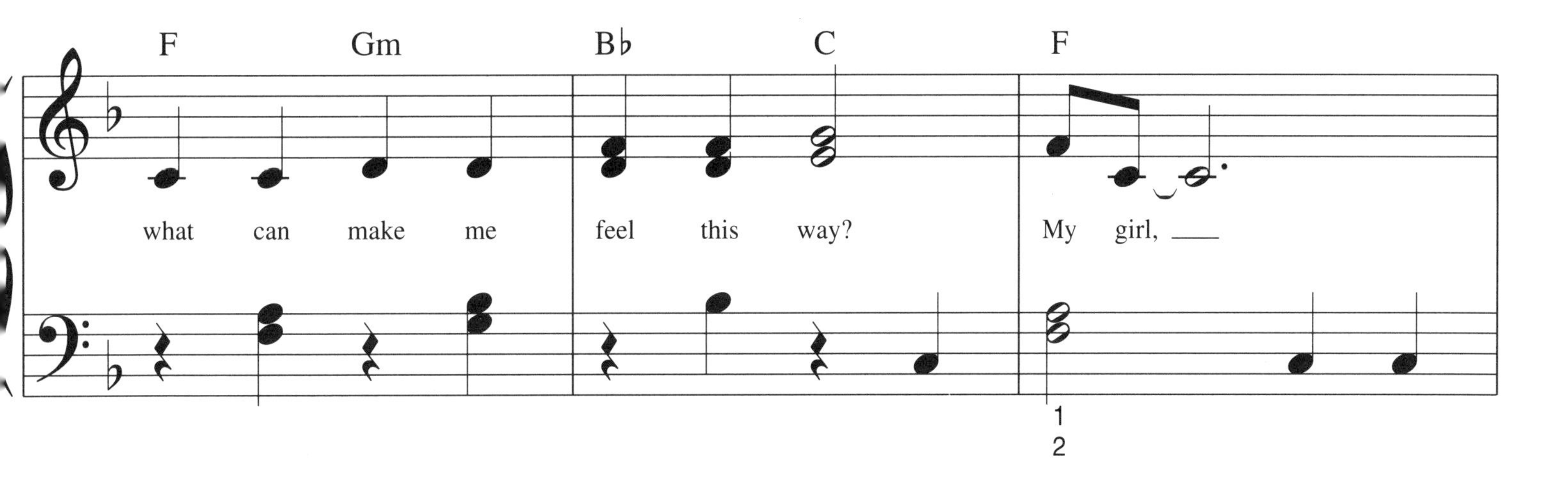
F
Gm
B♭
C
F
what can make me
feel this way?
My girl,
1
2

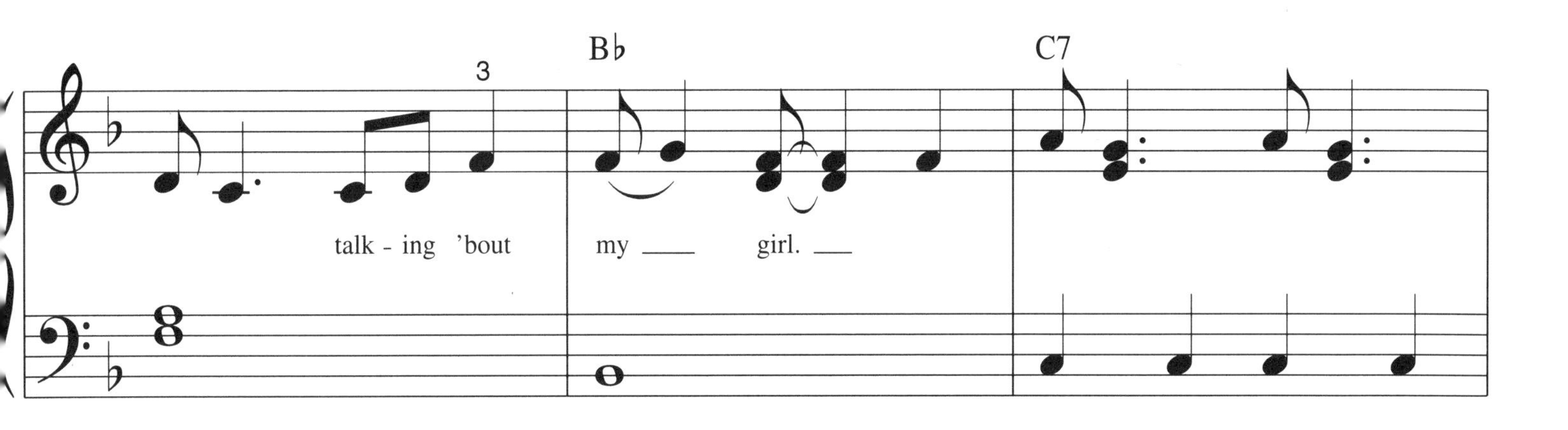
3
B♭
C7
talk - ing 'bout
my
girl.

F
Gm
I've got sun-shine on a cloud - y day with my girl. I've
1
2
C7
F
e - ven got the month of May with my girl.
Talk-ing 'bout,
Gm
C7sus
F
2
talk - ing 'bout, talk - ing 'bout my girl. Woo! My girl.
Gm
C7sus
F
That's all I can talk a - bout is my girl.
8

SIGNED, SEALED, DELIVERED I'M YOURS

Words and Music by STEVIE WONDER, SYREETA WRIGHT, LEE GARRETT and LULA MAE HARDAWAY

2.
C
Here I am
ba - by,
C7 F Dm7/G
you got my fu - ture in your hands.
C C7 F F7
Here I am
C C7 F Dm7
ba - by,
you got my fu - ture in your hands.

C
C7
F
F/G
I've done a lot of fool-ish things,
C
To Coda
F
C
a that I real - ly did - n't mean,
Hey, hey
Fmaj7
C
ba - by did - n't I,
Oh, ba - by,
3.
C
F
C
I'm yours.

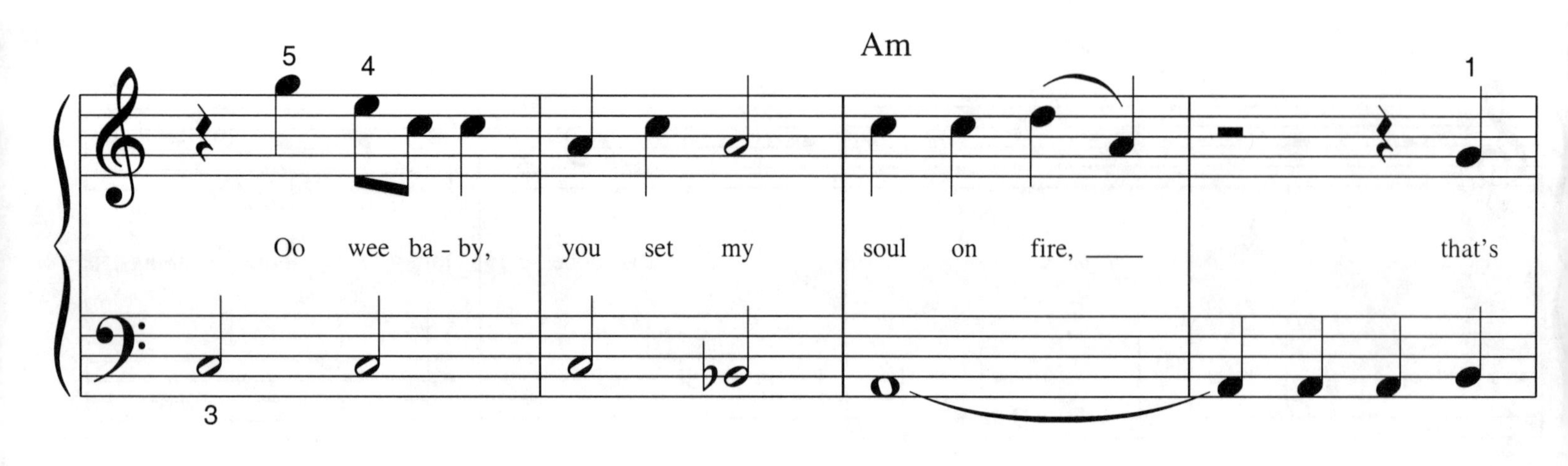
Am
Oo wee ba - by, you set my soul on fire, that's

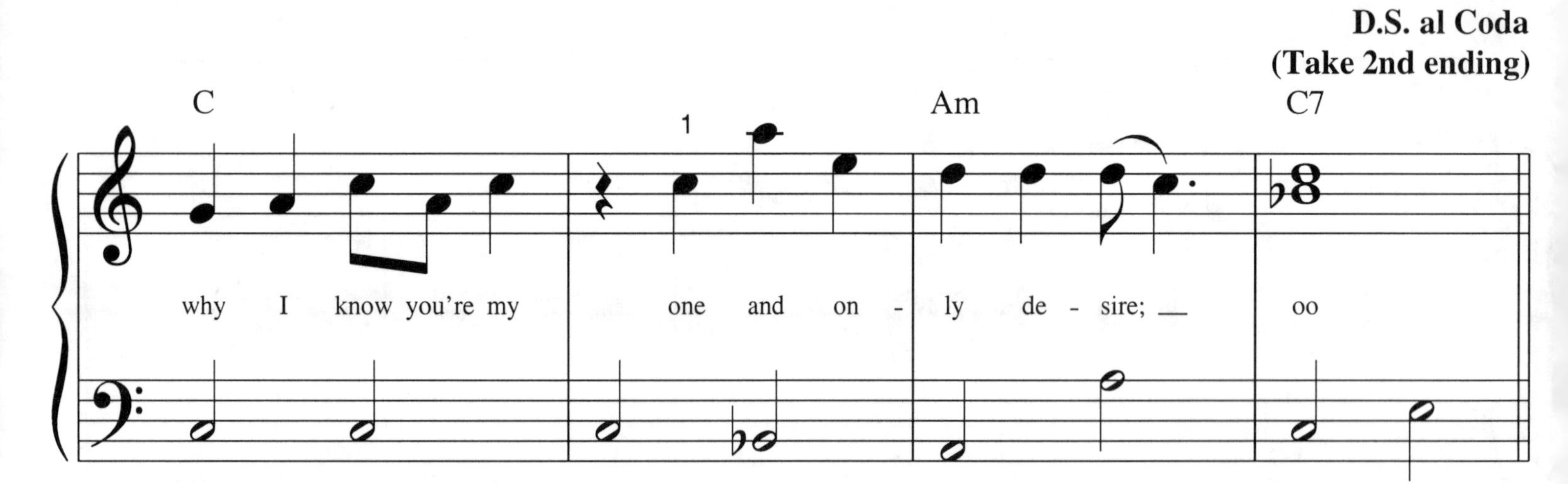
D.S. al Coda
(Take 2nd ending)
C
Am
C7
why I know you're my one and on - ly de - sire; oo

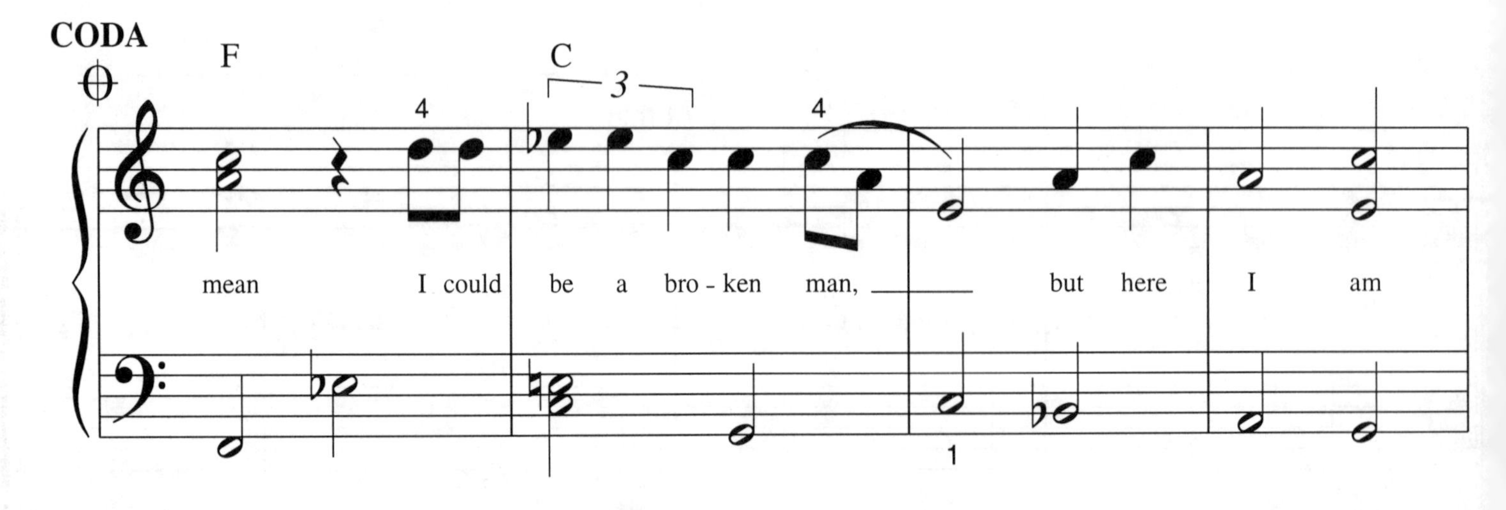
CODA
F
C
mean I could be a bro - ken man, but here I am

F
C
B♭
with your fu - ture, go your fu - ture, babe;

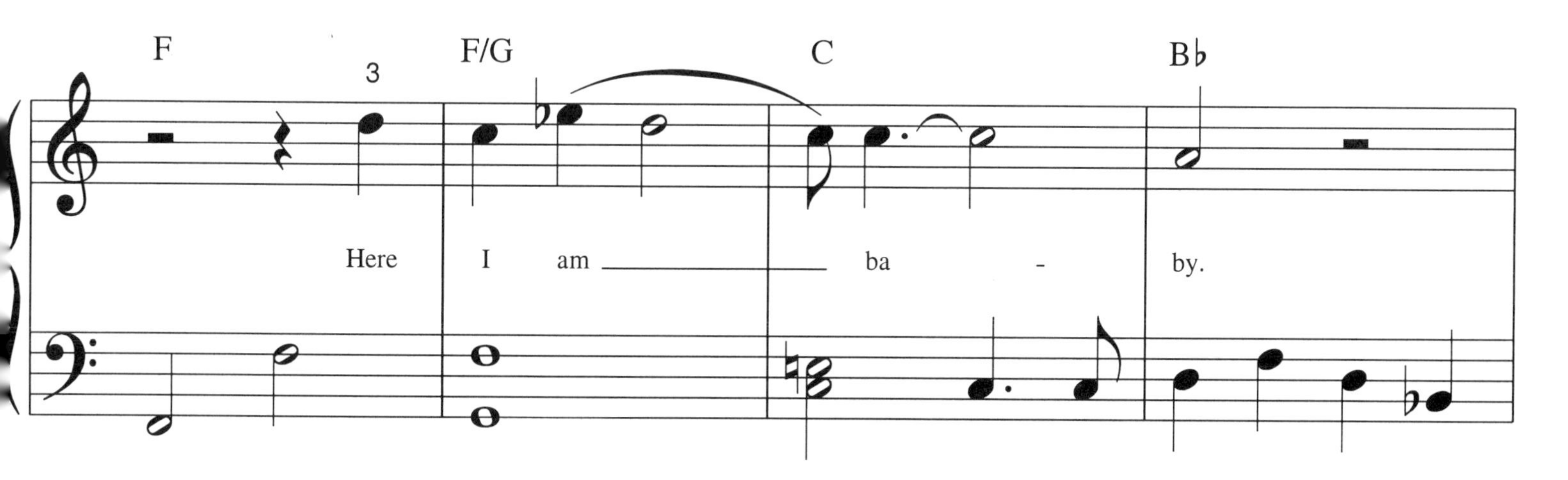

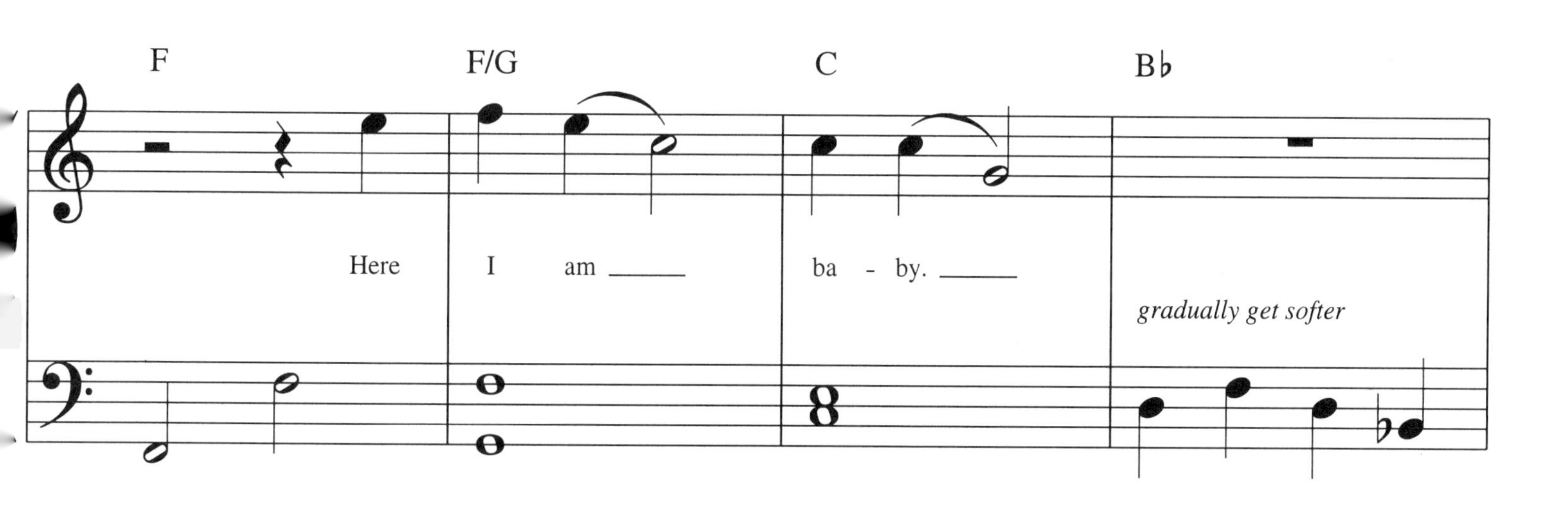

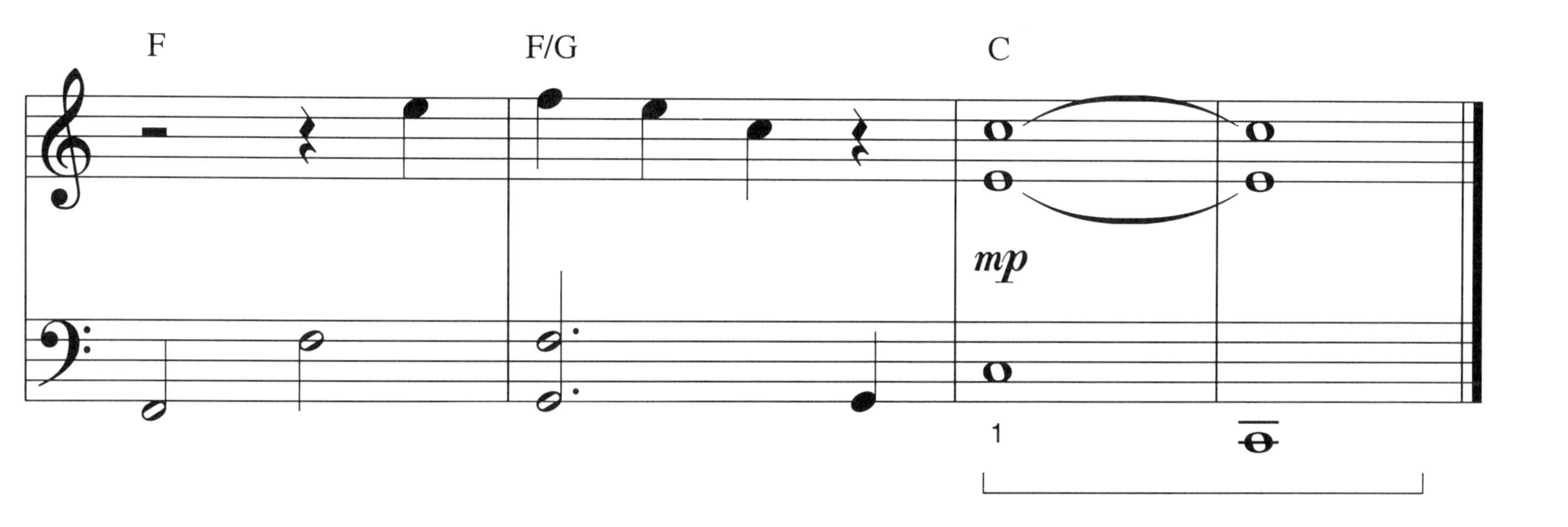

Additional Lyrics

2. Then that time I went and said goodbye
Now I'm back and not ashamed to cry, oo baby, here I am
Signed, sealed, delivered, I'm yours.

3. Seen a lot of things in this old world
When I touched them they did nothing girl, oo baby, here I am
Signed, sealed, delivered, I'm yours.

NEVER CAN SAY GOODBYE

Words and Music by Clifton Davis

Cmaj7
Gm7/C
tried and tried to hide my feel - ings they al - ways seem to

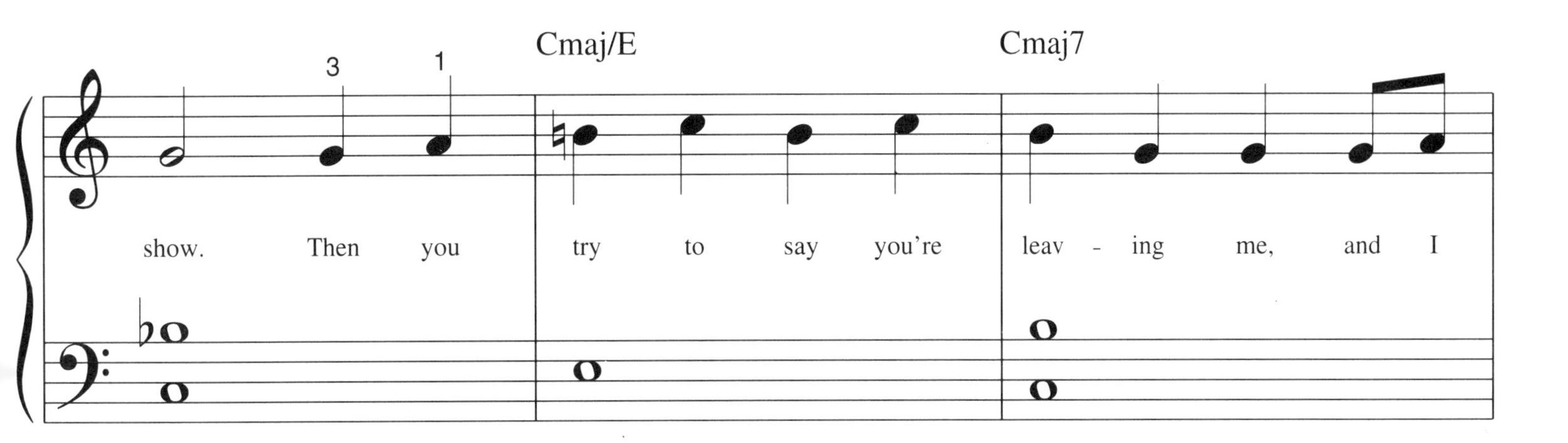
3
1
Cmaj/E
Cmaj7
show. Then you try to say you're leav - ing me, and I

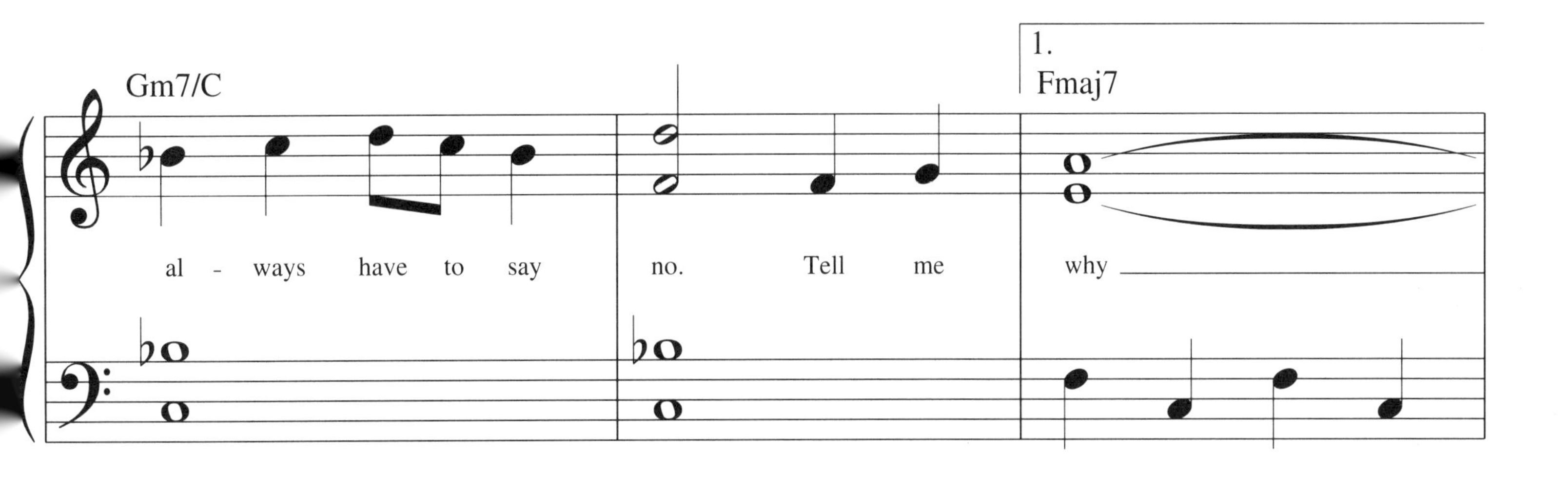
Gm7/C
1.
Fmaj7
al - ways have to say no. Tell me why

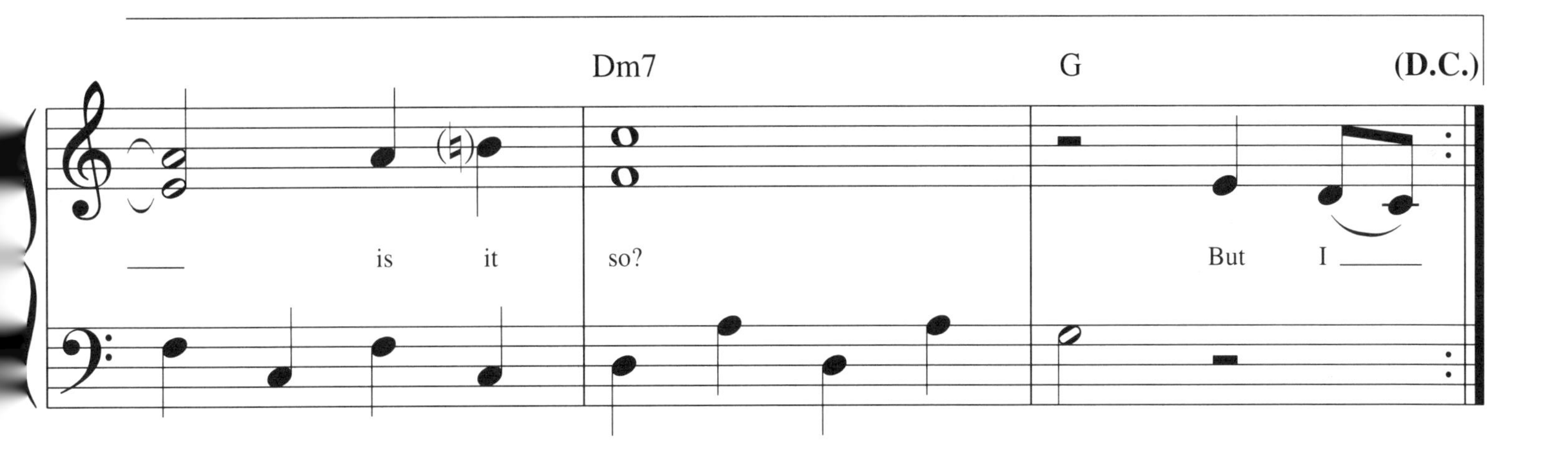
Dm7
G
(D.C.)
is it so? But I

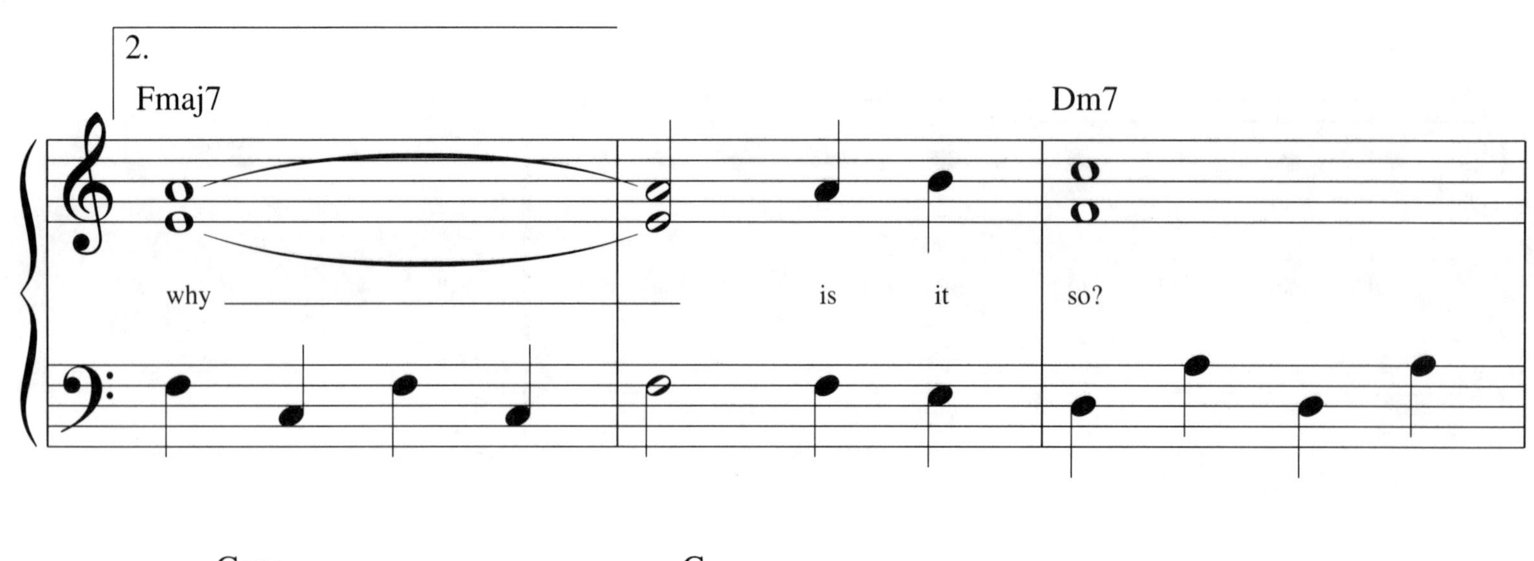
2.
Fmaj7
Dm7
why
is it
so?

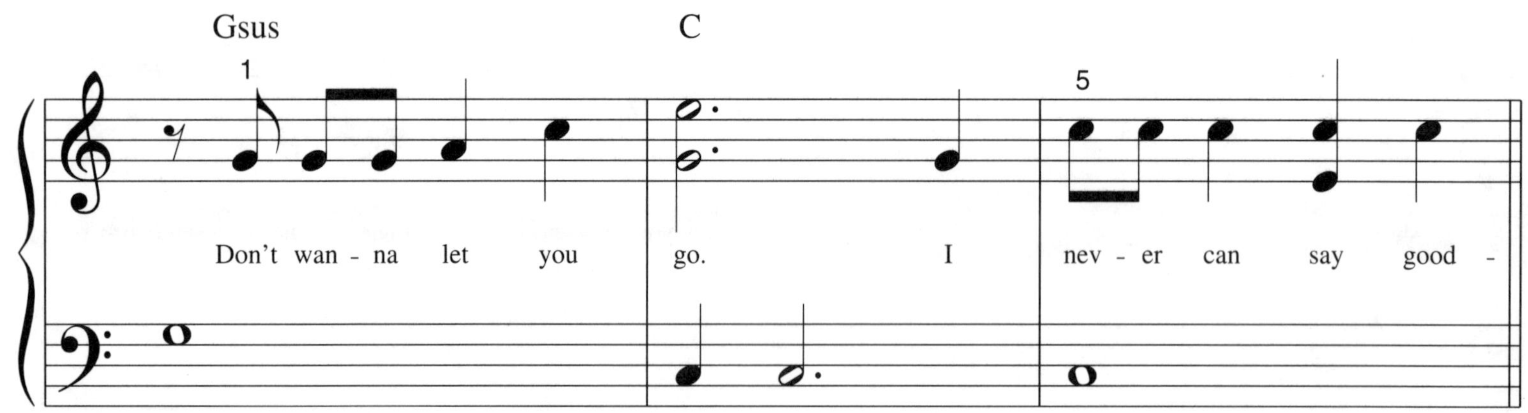
Gsus
C
1
5
Don't wan - na let you
go.
I
nev - er can say good -

Cm7
D7/C
bye, girl.
Don't wan - na let you
go.
I

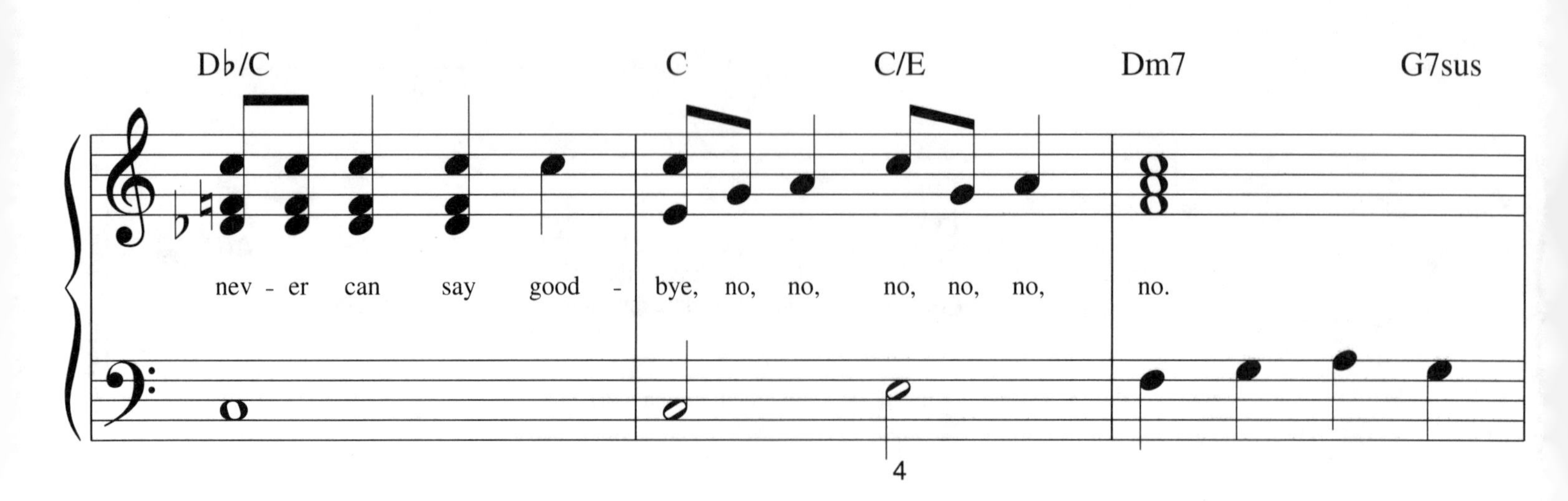
D♭/C
C
C/E
Dm7
G7sus
nev - er can say good -
bye, no, no, no, no, no,
no.
4

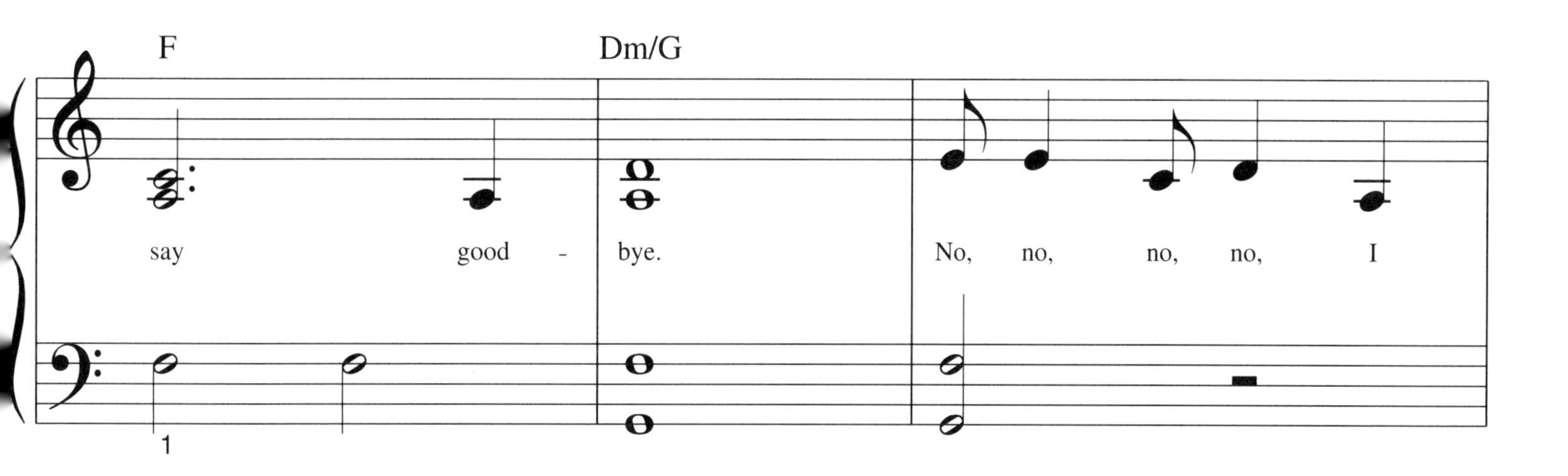

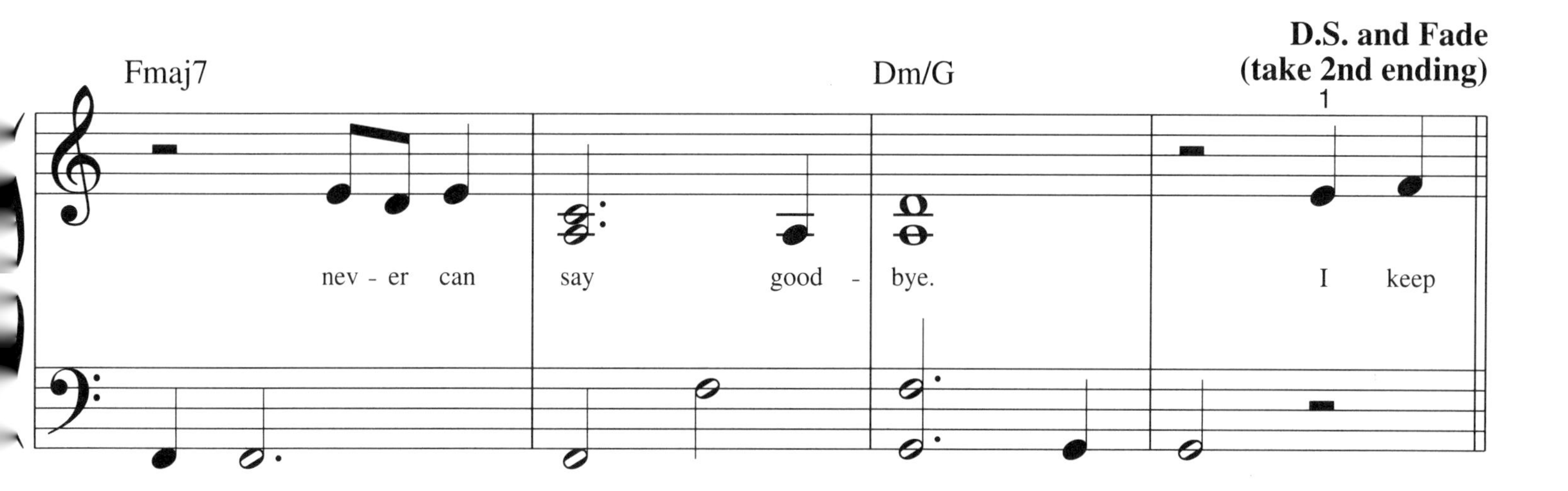

Additional Lyrics

2. Ev'ry time I think I've had enough and start heading for the door,
There's very strange vibrations, piercing me right to the core. It says
Turn around you fool you know you love her more and more.

3. I keep thinkin' that our problems soon are all gonna work out,
But there's that same unhappy feelin', there's that anguish, there's that
Doubt. It's that same old dizzy hang-up can't do with you or without.

STOP! IN THE NAME OF LOVE

Words and Music by LAMONT DOZIER,
BRIAN HOLLAND and EDWARD HOLLAND

F
5
I watch you walk
G7
down the street,
F
Know - ing your oth - er
G7
love you meet,
C
2
But this time be - fore you
G/B
run to her
4
F
leav - ing me a -
3
lone to cry.
2
C F
1
Have - n't I been
C
good to you?
F
5
Have - n't I been
C Am
sweet to you?

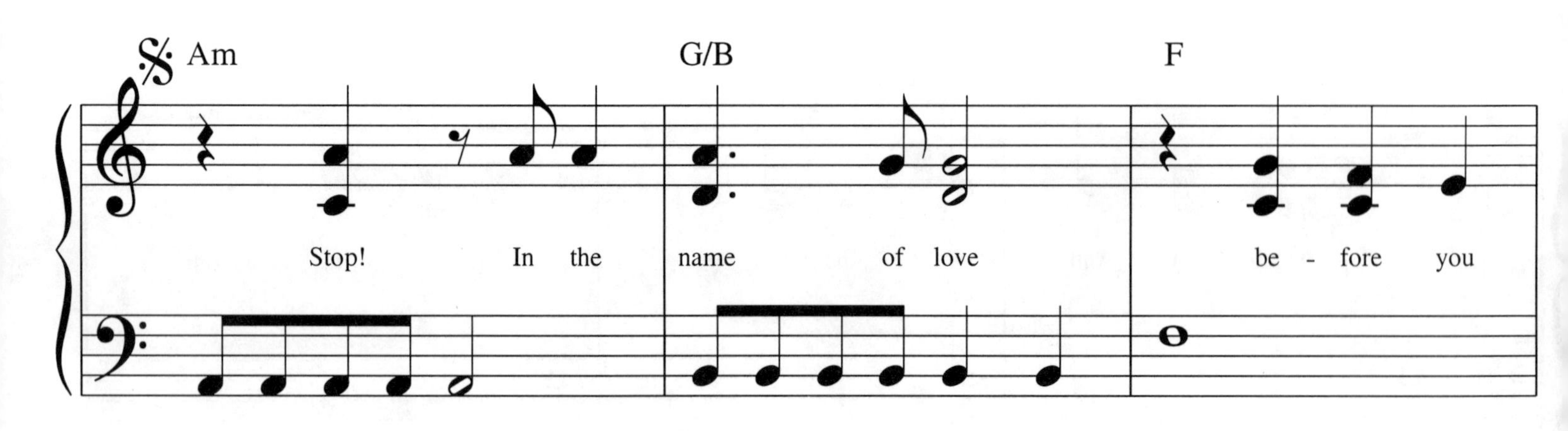

Am
G/B
F
Stop! In the name of love be - fore you

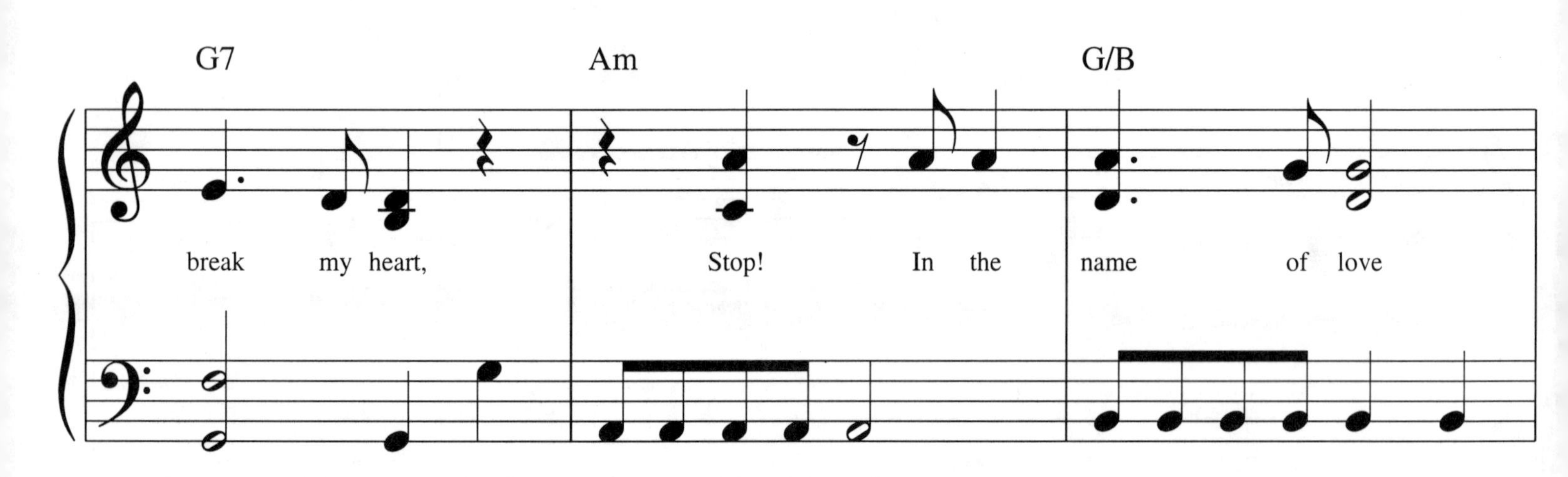

G7
Am
G/B
break my heart, Stop! In the name of love

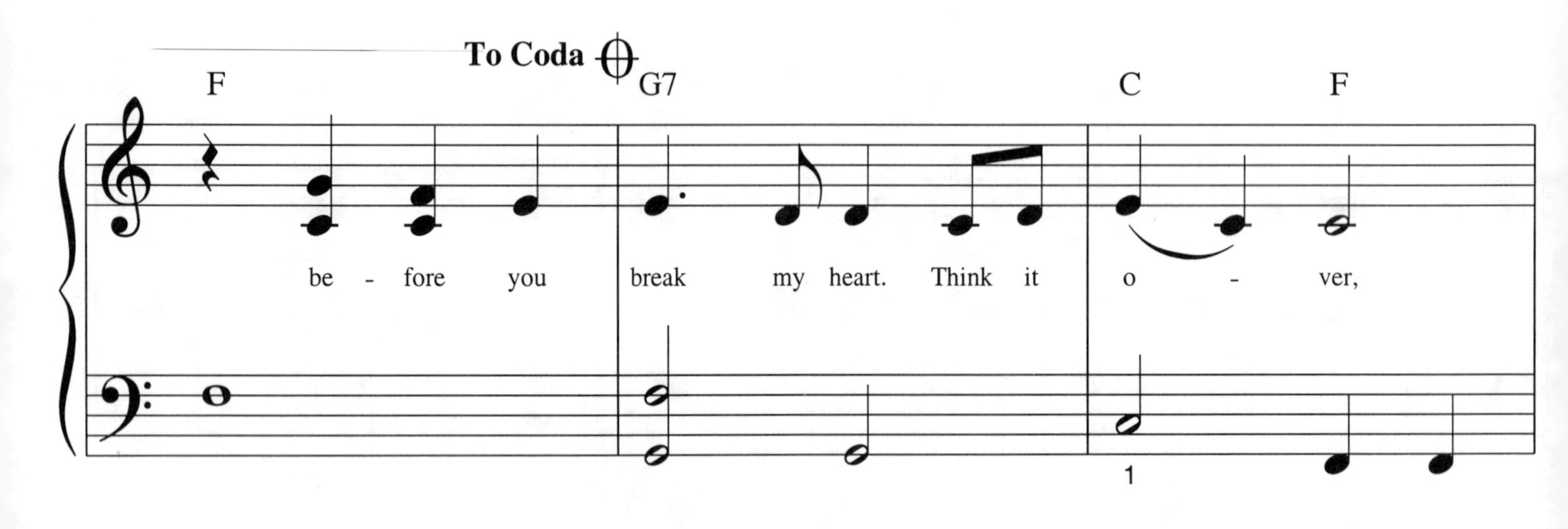

To Coda
F
G7
C
F
be - fore you break my heart. Think it o - ver,
1

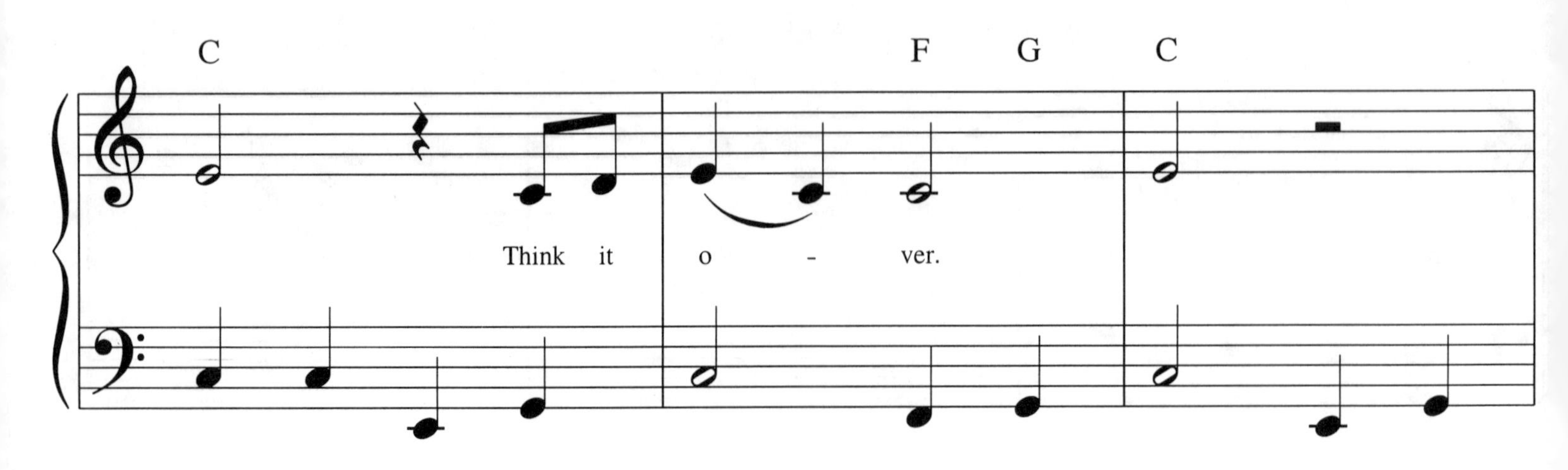

C
F
G
C
Think it o - ver.

1.
Em/B
2
I've known of your,
your se - clud - ed nights,

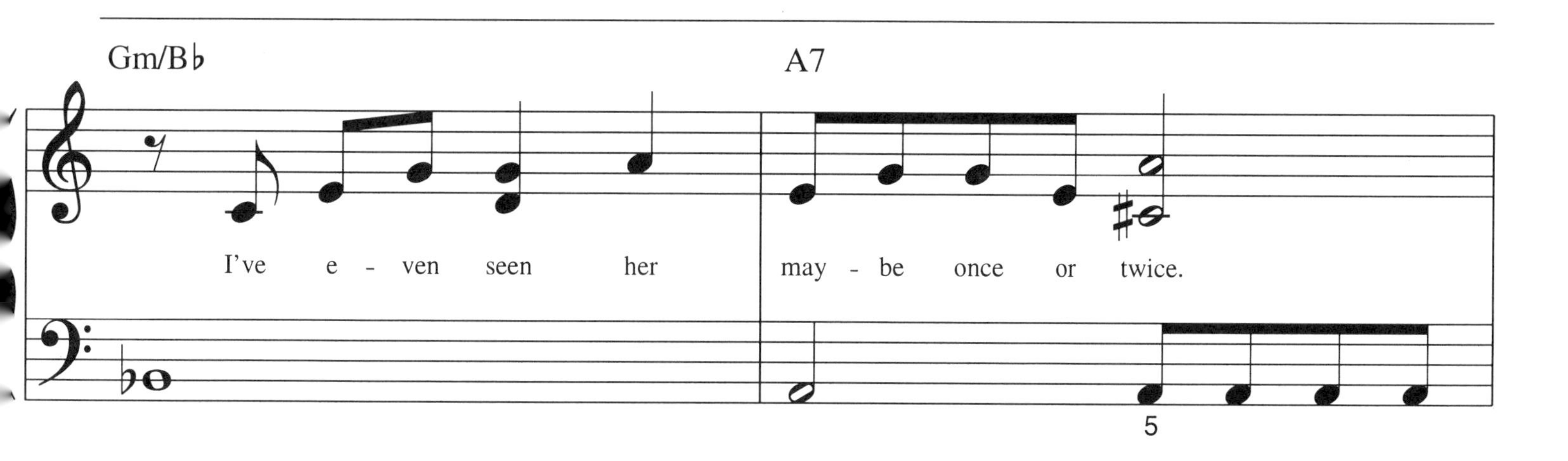
Gm/B♭
A7
I've e - ven seen her
may - be once or twice.
5

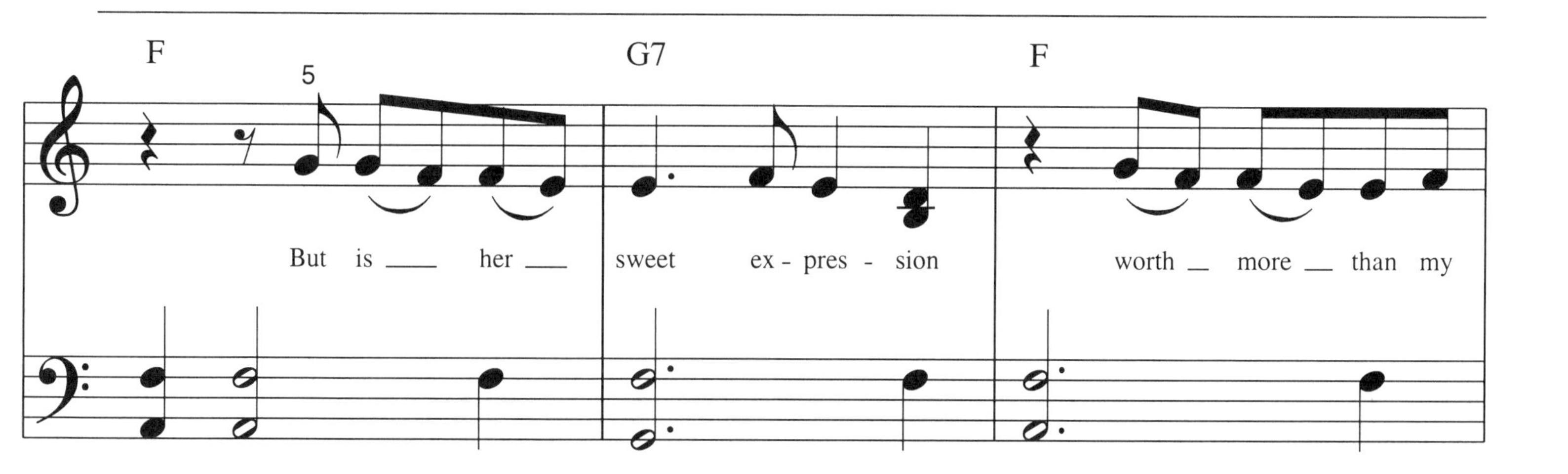
F
G7
F
5
But is her
sweet ex - pres - sion
worth more than my

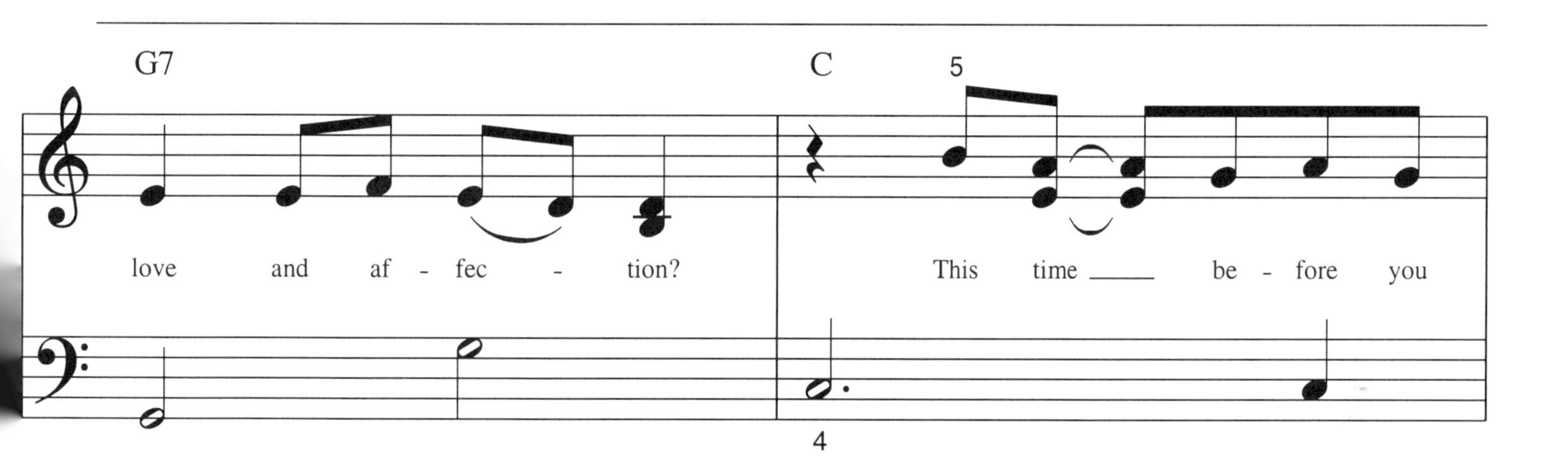
G7
C
5
love and af - fec - tion?
This time be - fore you
4

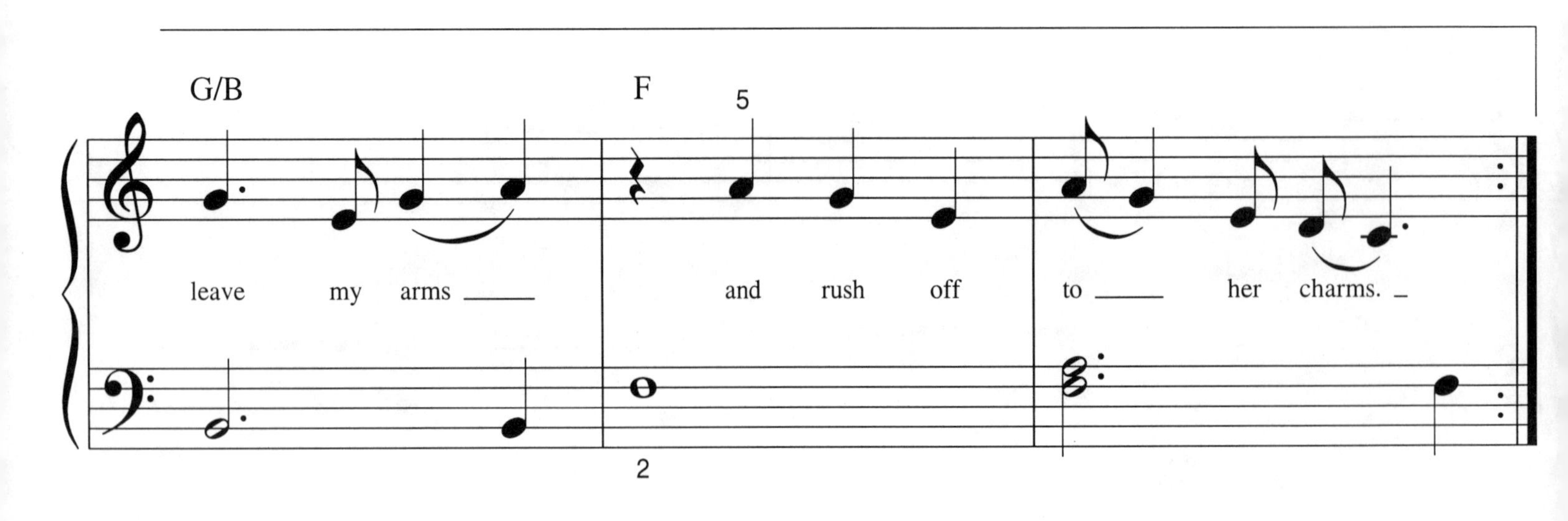
G/B
F
leave my arms
and rush off
to her charms.

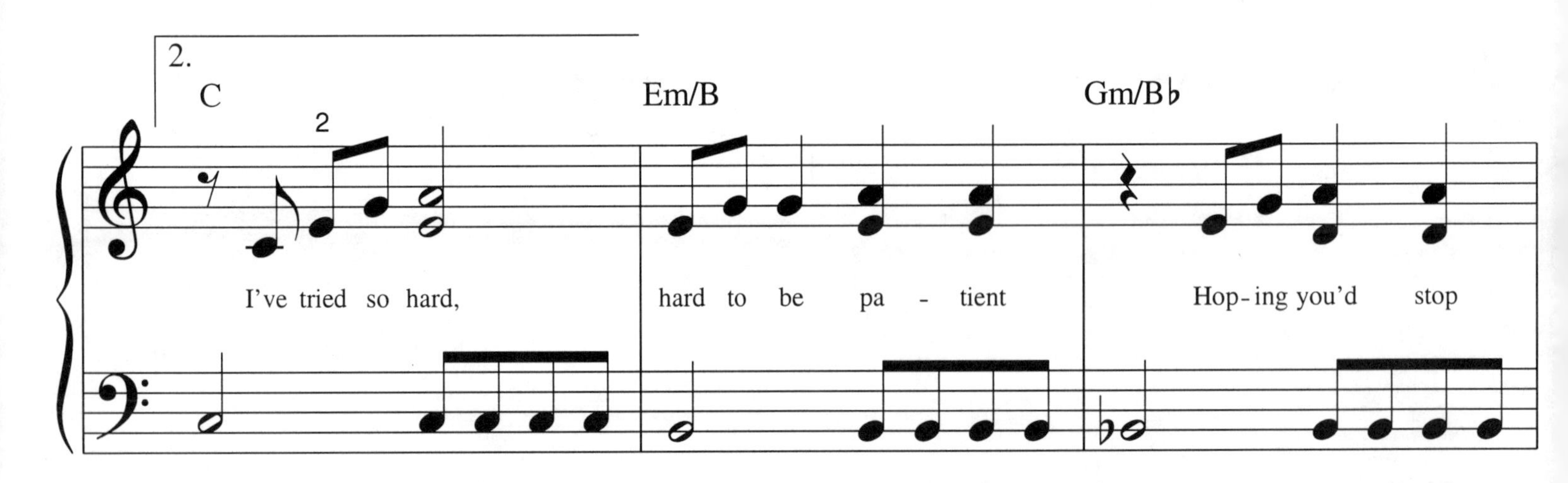
2.
C
Em/B
Gm/B♭
I've tried so hard,
hard to be pa - tient
Hop-ing you'd stop

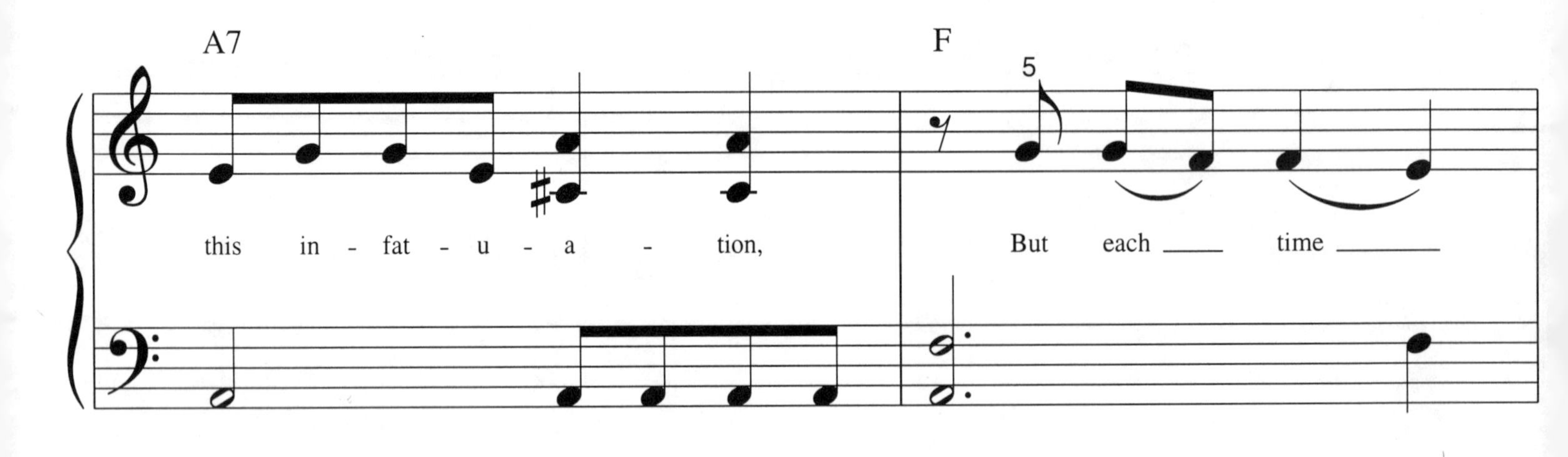
A7
F
this in - fat - u - a - tion,
But each time

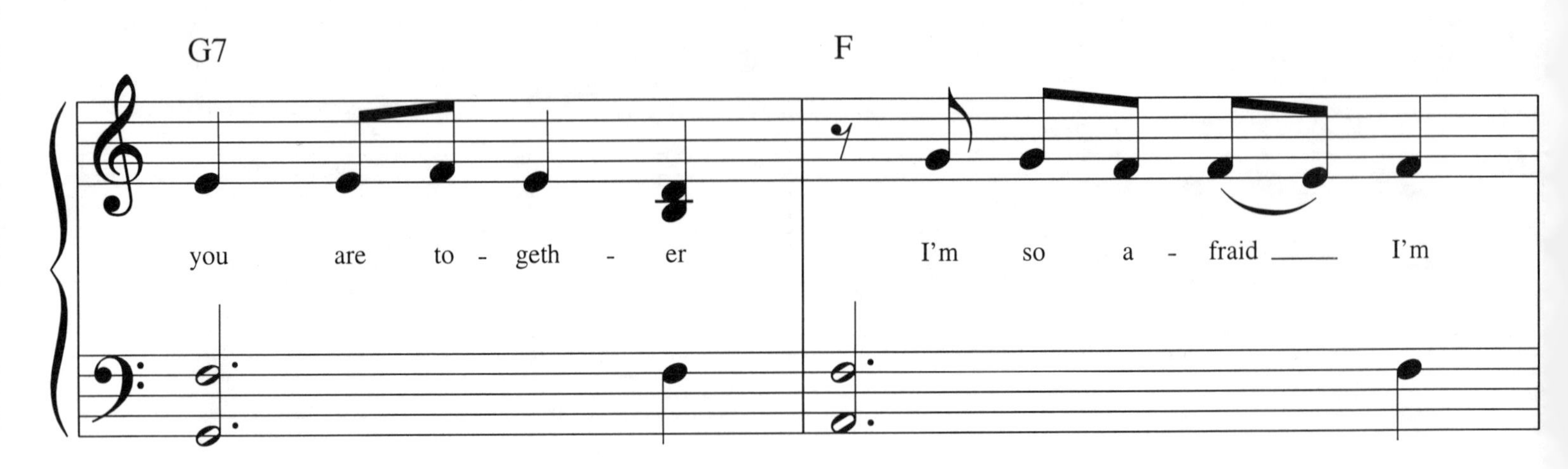
G7
F
you are to - geth - er
I'm so a - fraid I'm

G7
D.S. al Coda
los - ing you for - ev - er.
CODA
G7
break my heart;
Am
G/B
F
Stop! In the name of love Be - fore you
G7
C
F
C
break my heart.
5
3
F
G
C

THREE TIMES A LADY

Words and Music by
LIONEL RICHIE

F/E♭
Dm
A7♯5
A7
must ___ say out
loud: ___
You're
F
C/E
E♭
B♭/F
once,
twice,
three times a
la - dy
5
Gm7
F
C
C/B♭
and I
love ___
you.
Yes, you're
F
C/E
E♭
B♭/F
once,
twice,
three times a
la - dy,

Gm7
F
C
C/B♭
and I love you,
C/A
C/G
F
C/F
I love you.
B♭/F
B♭/C
F
C/F
When we are to - geth - er, the
B♭/F
B♭/C
F
C/F
mo - ments I cher - ish with ev - 'ry beat of my

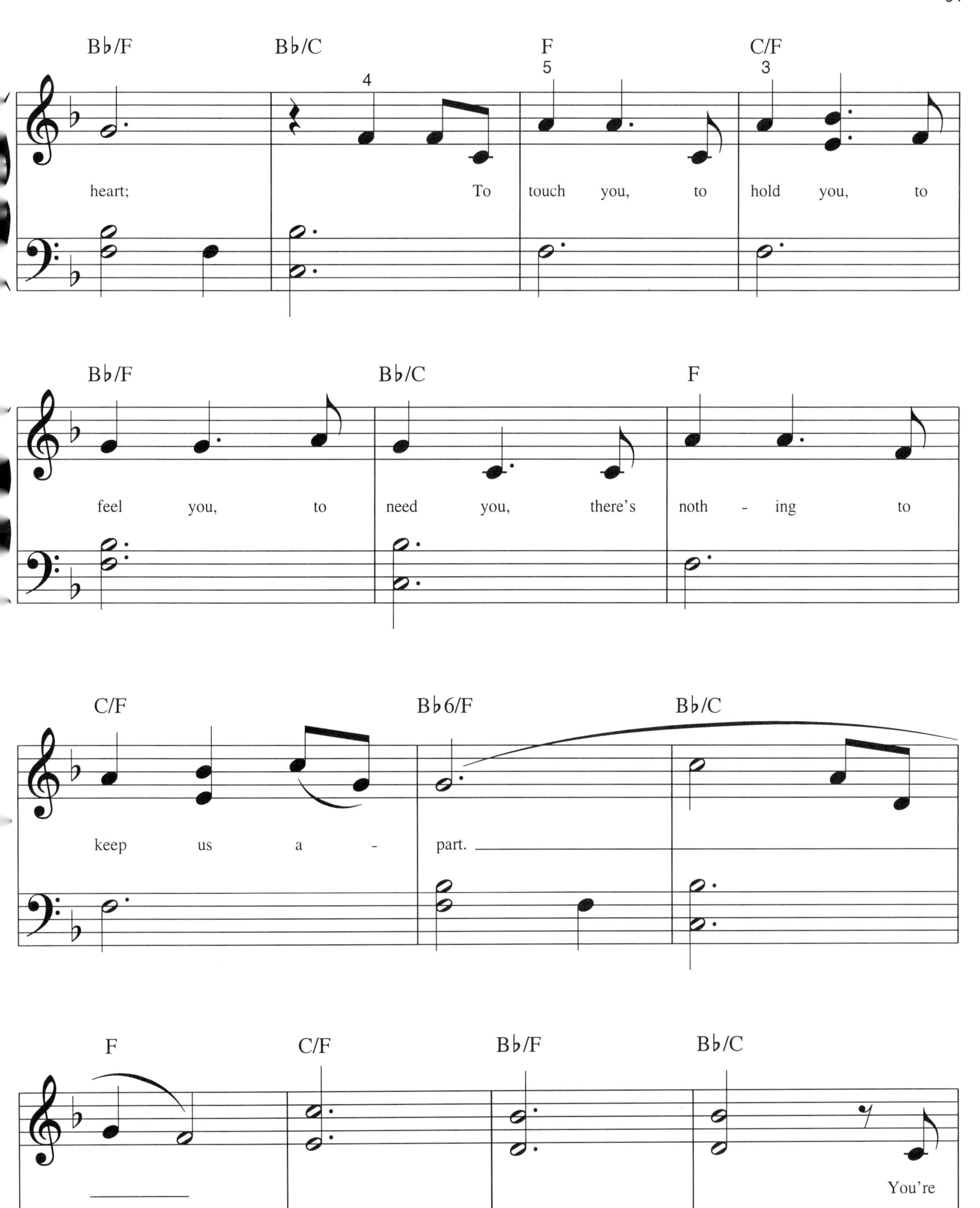
B♭/F
B♭/C
F
C/F
4
5
3
heart; To touch you, to hold you, to
B♭/F
B♭/C
F
feel you, to need you, there's noth - ing to
C/F
B♭6/F
B♭/C
keep us a - part.
F
C/F
B♭/F
B♭/C
You're

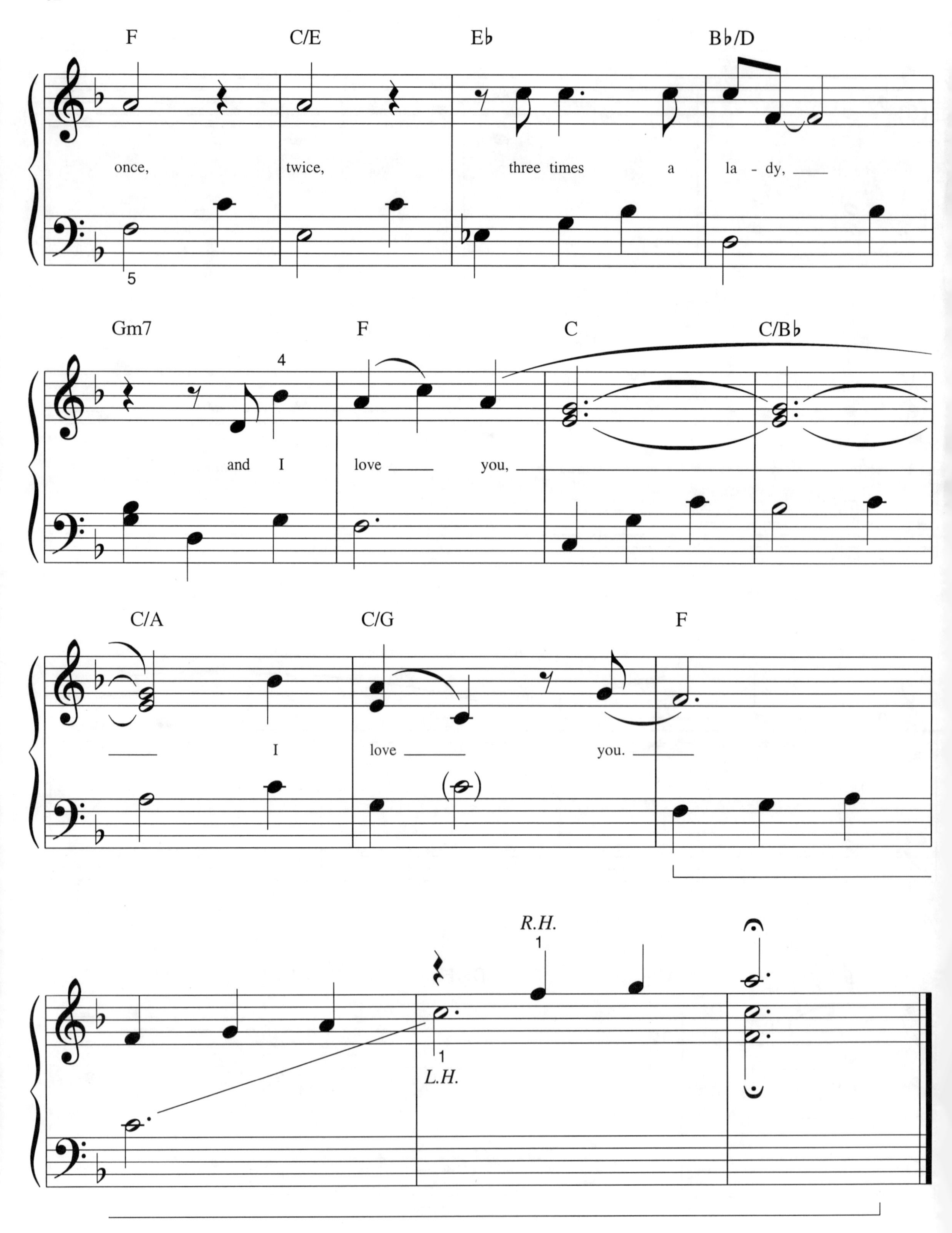
F
C/E
E♭
B♭/D
once,
twice,
three times
a
la - dy,
5
Gm7
F
C
C/B♭
4
and I
love
you,
C/A
C/G
F
I
love
you.
R.H.
1
1
L.H.

THE TRACKS OF MY TEARS

Words and Music by William "Smokey" Robinson,
Warren Moore and Marvin Tarplin

G
C
F
1
face; you'll see my smile looks out of
face, oh, you'll see my smile looks out of
G
C
F
place. If you look clos - er, it's eas - y to
place. A - look a lit - tle bit clos - er, it's eas - y to
3
G
C
F
C
2
trace the tracks of my tears. I need
trace the tracks of my tears. Oh,
1.
2.
F
C
F
C (D.C.)
F
C
3
you, need you.
need you.

F C F C
Hey, hey, yeah. (Out -
C/F F C C/F C
side) I'm mas - que - rad - ing (In - side) my hope is
F C C/F C F C
fad - ing; a (Just a clown) oo, yeah a - since you put me down. My
D.S. and Fade
Dm C G
smile is my make - up I wear since my break - up with you. Ba - by, take a

WHERE DID OUR LOVE GO

Words and Music by BRIAN HOLLAND,
LAMONT DOZIER and EDWARD HOLLAND

Moderate Rock Shuffle

C G

1.,3. Ba - by, ba - by, ba - by, don't leave me.
2. Ba - by, ba - by, where did our love go?

mf

Dm7

Ooh, please don't leave me all by my - self.
And all of your prom - is - es of a love for - ev - er - more!

G F C

I've ___ got this burn - ing, burn - ing,

G

yearn - ing feel - in' in - side me. Ooh, deep in -

Dm
G
To Coda
side me
and it hurts so
bad.

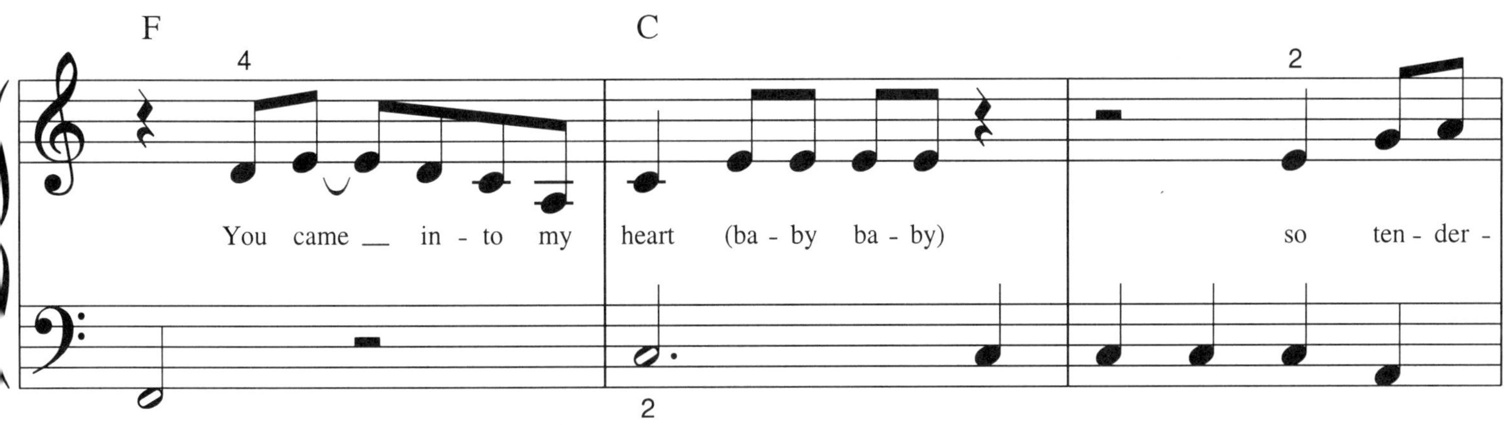
F
C
You came in - to my
heart (ba - by ba - by)
so ten - der -

G
Dm7
ly
with a burn - ing
love (ba - by ba - by)

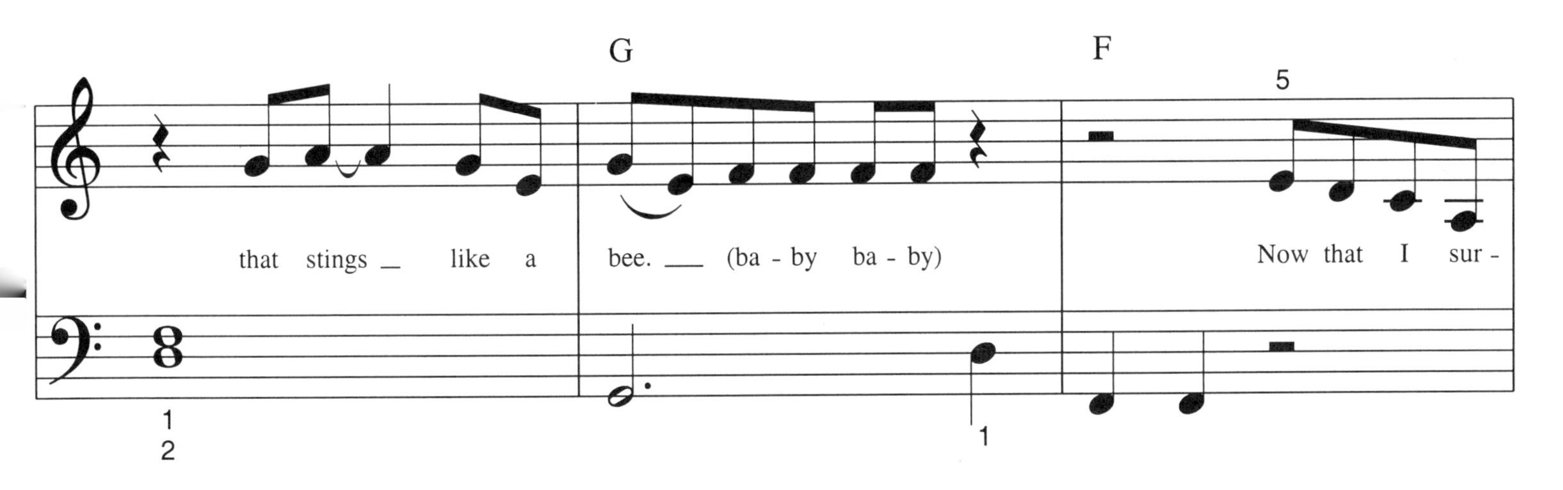
G
F
that stings like a
bee. (ba - by ba - by)
Now that I sur -

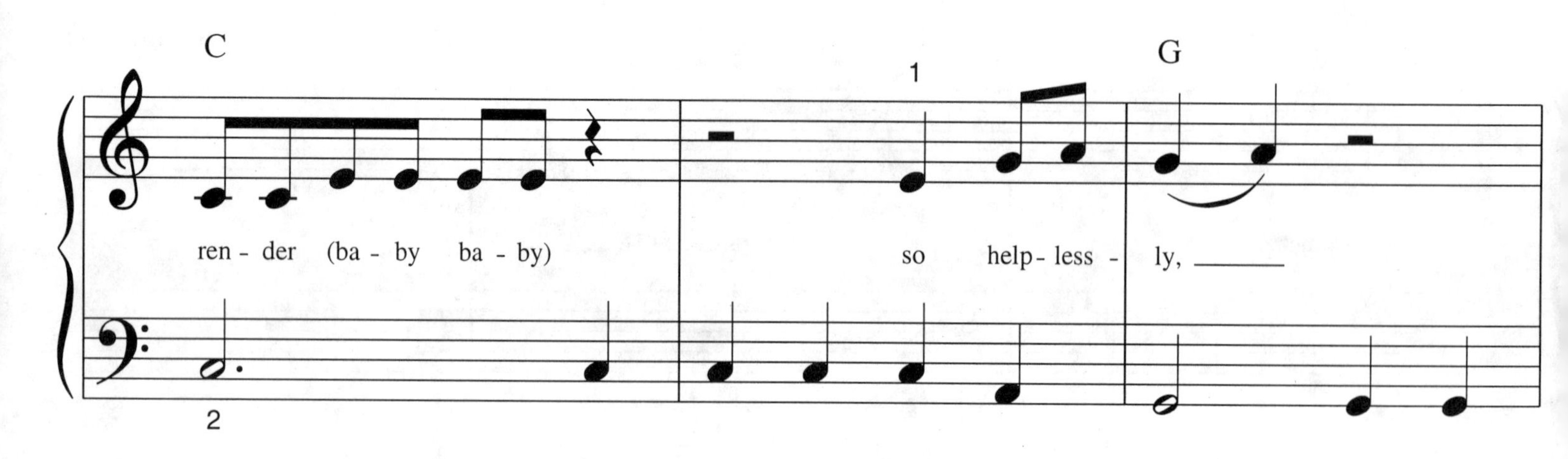
C
G
ren - der (ba - by ba - by)
so help - less - ly,

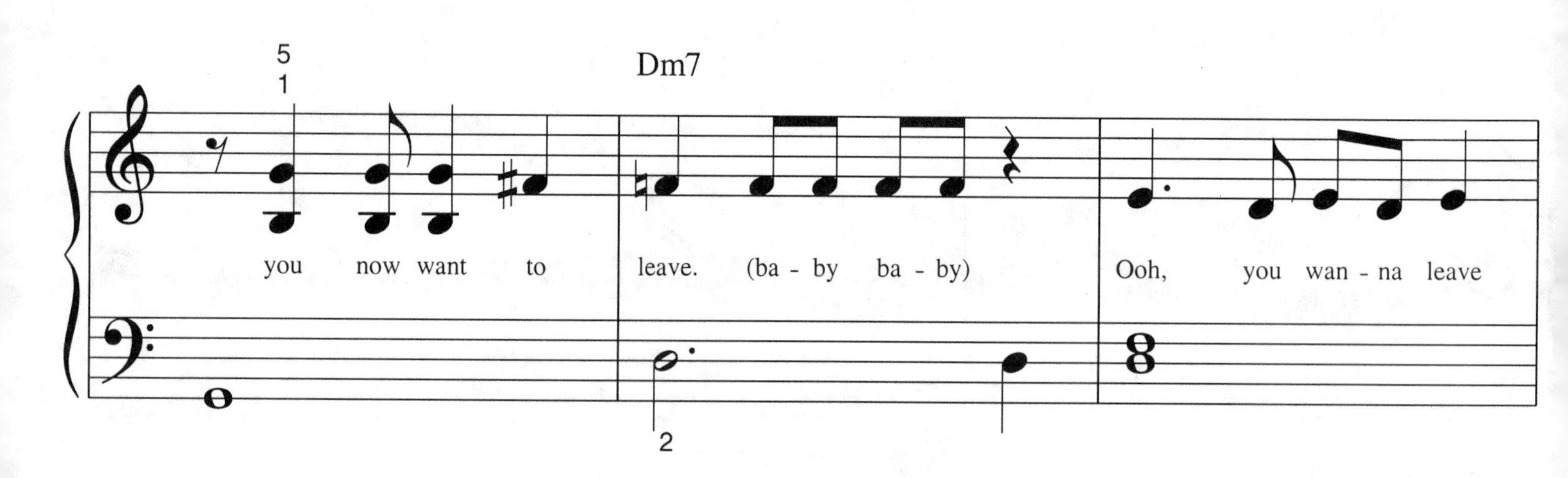
Dm7
you now want to
leave. (ba - by ba - by)
Ooh, you wan - na leave

G
F
C
me. (ba - by ba - by)
Ooh, (ba - by ba - by)
ba - by, ba - by,

G
where did our
love go?
Ooh, don't you

Dm7
G7
want me?
Don't you want me no
more? (ba - by ba - by)
F
D.C. al Coda
(2nd time)
Ooh, ba - by.
CODA
F
C
Be - fore you won my
heart, (ba - by ba - by)
G
Dm
you were a per-fect
guy.
But now that you
got me,
G N.C.
you wan - na leave me be -
hind. (ba - by ba - by)
Ooh, ba - by.

C
G
Ba - by, ba - by,
ba - by, don't
leave me.
Ooh, please don't

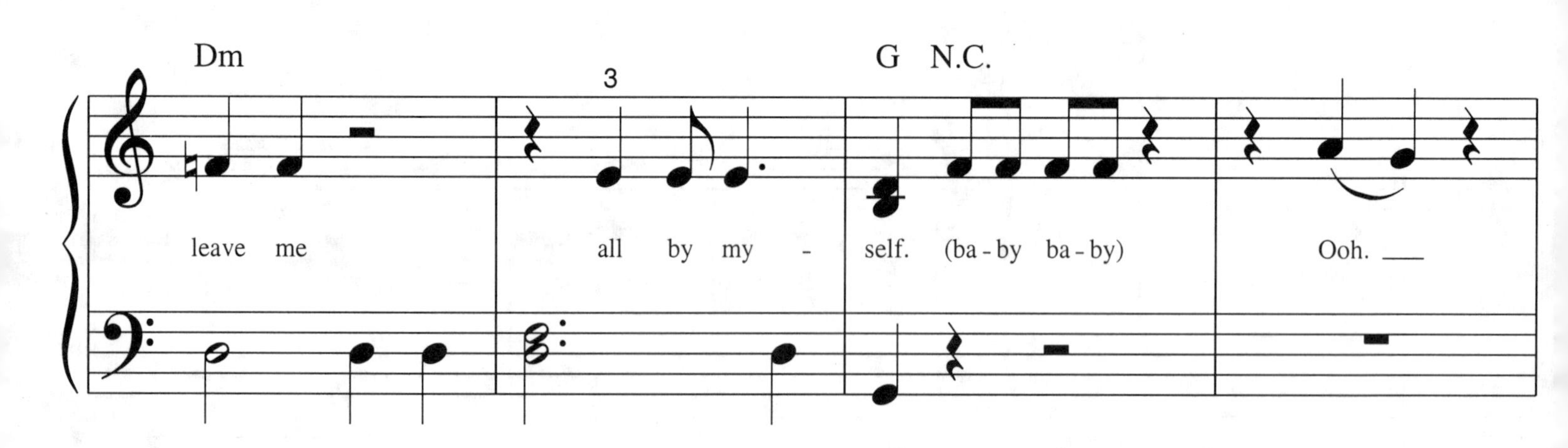

Dm
3
G N.C.
leave me
all by my - self. (ba - by ba - by)
Ooh.

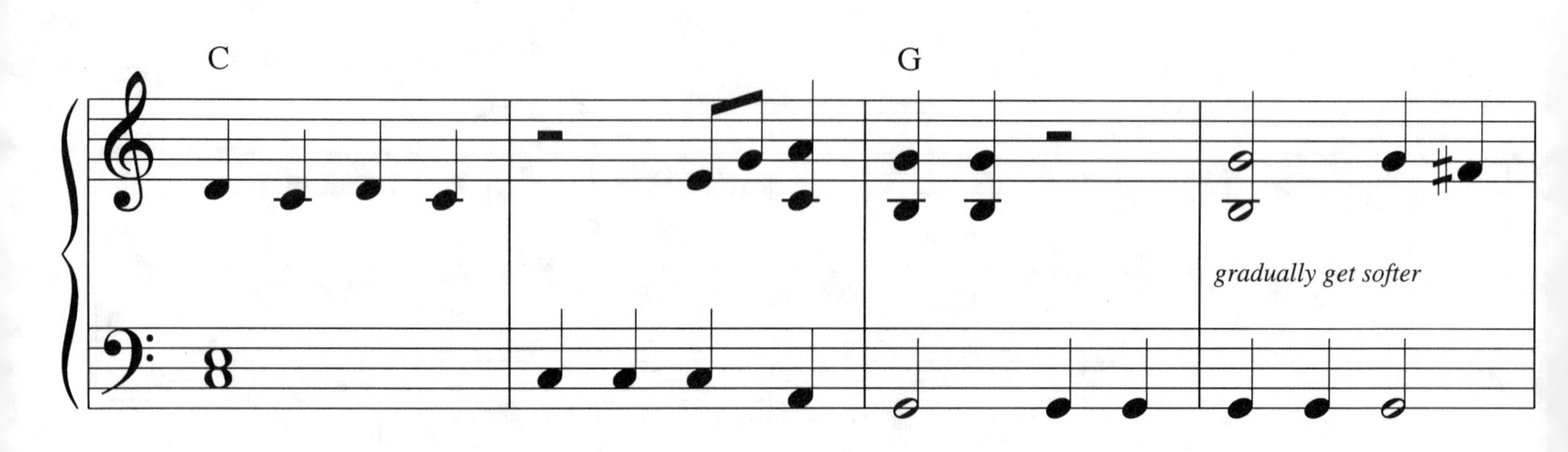

C
G
gradually get softer

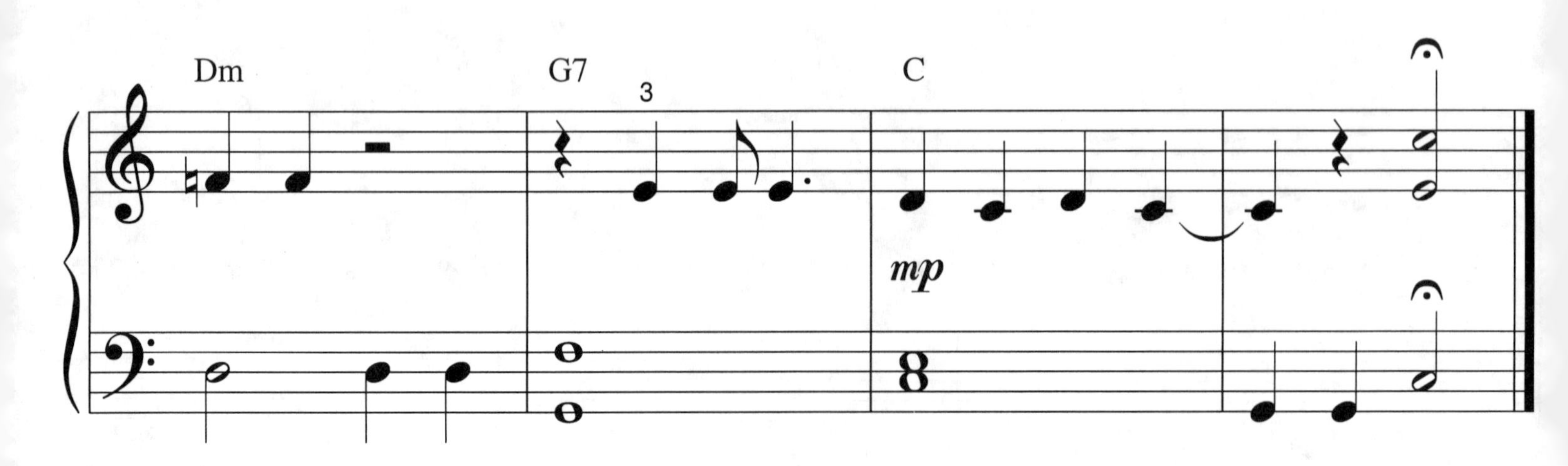

Dm
G7
3
C
mp

YOU ARE THE SUNSHINE OF MY LIFE

Words and Music by
STEVIE WONDER

Am7
Abm7
Gm7
eye.
For - ev - er
Bb/C
C7
F
To Coda
Bb
Bb/C
F
you'll stay in my
heart.
I feel like
You must have
Gm7
C7
Am7
Gm7
C7
this is the be - gin - ning,
known that I was lone - ly,
F
Gm7
C7
Em7/B
'though I've loved you for a mil - lion years.
be - cause you came to my res - cue.

A11 A7 D Em7 A7
And if I thought our love was
and I know that this must be
Dm G7
end - ing, I'd find my - self
heav - en; how could so much love
C7 Gm7 C7
D.S. al Coda (2nd time)
drown - ing in my own tears. Whoa, whoa.
be in - side of you? Whoa, whoa.
CODA
B♭ B♭/C Fmaj7

YOU KEEP ME HANGIN' ON

Words and Music by EDWARD HOLLAND,
LAMONT DOZIER and BRIAN HOLLAND

Em/G
Em7/D
Am/F
Am/E
3
need me but you keep me hang - in' on.
1.
B♭/C
5
1
F/C
Why do you keep a com - in' a - round play - ing with my
C
B♭/C
heart? Why don't - cha get out of my life
F/C
C
G
4
2
and let me make a new start? Let me get o - ver you the
1

E
Am/E
2.
B♭/C
5
1
way you've got - ten o - ver
me.
You say al - though
F/C
C
we broke up you
still wan - na be just
friends.
B♭/C
F/C
4
But how can we
still be friends when
see - ing you on - ly breaks my
A
E
heart a - gain.
Spoken: And there ain't noth - ing I can
do a - bout it.

A
Em/G
Em7/D
5
4
Set me free why don't-cha ba - by. Get out my life why
Am/F
Am/E
B♭/C
F/C
don't-cha ba - by. You claim you still care for me but your
C
B♭/C
heart and soul needs to be free. Now that you've
F/C
C
got your free-dom you wan - na still hold on to me.
1

G
E
4
You don't want me
for your-self
so
let me find some-bod - y
Am/E
A
Em/G
else.
Why don't - cha be a
man a - bout it
Em7/D
5
3
Am/F
Am/E
A
and set me
free.
Now
you don't care a
Em/G
Em7/D
Am/F
Am/E
thing a - bout me.
You're just us - ing
me.
Boy,

A
Em/G
Em7/D
get out, get
out - ta my life
and let me sleep at
Am/F
Am/E
A
Em/G
3
night.
'Cause you don't real - ly
love me, you just
Em7/D
Am/F
Am/E
A
keep me hang - ing
on.
'Cause you don't real - ly
Am/E
Em/G
F
Am
need me, so
let me be,
set me free.
gradually get softer
mp
rit.

Big Fun With Big-Note Piano Books!

These songbooks feature exciting easy arrangements for beginning piano students.

Broadway Classics
Bill Boyd

12 broadway favorites for big note piano, including: Don't Cry For Me Argentina • Give My Regards To Broadway • If I Were A Rich Man • Memory • The Sound Of Music • and more.

00290180 .... $7.95

Broadway Favorites
Bill Boyd

12 Broadway favorites for big-note piano, including: All I Ask Of You • Edelweiss • Everything's Coming Up Roses • I Dreamed A Dream • Sunrise, Sunset • and more!

00290184 .... $7.95

Children's Favorites
14 songs children love, including: The Brady Bunch • Casper the Friendly Ghost • Going to the Zoo • The Grouch Song • Hakuna Matata • The Name Game • The Siamese Cat Song • Winnie the Pooh • more.

00310282 .... $7.95

A Christmas Collection
33 simplified favorites, including: The Christmas Song (Chestnuts Roasting) • Frosty The Snow Man • A Holly Jolly Christmas • I Saw Mommy Kissing Santa Claus • Mister Santa • The Most Wonderful Day Of The Year • Nuttin' For Christmas • Silver Bells • and more.

00221818 .... $10.95

Contemporary Favorites
Bill Boyd

12 pop hits, including: Don't Worry, Be Happy • The Rainbow Connection • Under The Boardwalk • and more.

00290179 .... $7.95

Country Favorites
28 songs, including: Achy Breaky Heart • Down At The Twist & Shout • God Bless The U.S.A. • Your Cheatin' Heart • and more.

00222554 .... $10.95

Disney Movie Magic
Big-note arrangements of 12 Disney movie songs: Arabian Nights • Beauty and the Beast • Circle of Life • Colors of the Wind • God Help the Outcasts • Hakuna Matata • Kiss the Girl • Part of Your World • Someday • Something There • A Whole New World • more.

00310194 .... $10.95

Great Jazz Standards
arranged by Bill Boyd

20 songs, including: April In Paris • Don't Get Around Much Anymore • How High The Moon • It Don't Mean A Thing (If It Ain't Got That Swing) • When I Fall In Love • and more.

00222575 .... $12.95

Hymn Favorites
Includes 20 favorite hymns: Abide With Me • Blest Be The Tie That Binds • Jesus Loves Me • Nearer My God To Thee • Rock Of Ages • What A Friend We Have In Jesus • and more.

00221802 .... $6.95

Les Misérables
14 songs, including: At The End Of The Day • Bring Him Home • Castle On A Cloud • Do You Hear The People Sing • I Dreamed A Dream • In My Life • On My Own • and more.

00221812 .... $12.95

Disney's The Lion King
A great easy-to-play souvenir folio featuring full-color art from the movie and 5 songs: Circle Of Life • I Just Can't Wait To Be King • Be Prepared • Hakuna Matata • Can You Feel The Love Tonight.

00221819 .... $14.95

Movie Hits
21 songs popularized on the silver screen, including: Beauty And The Beast • Don't Worry Be Happy • Endless Love • The Rainbow Connection • Somewhere Out There • Tears In Heaven • Unchained Melody • Under The Sea • A Whole New World • and more.

00221804 .... $9.95

Patriotic Gems
arr. Bill Boyd

20 American classics, including: America • America, The Beautiful • Battle Hymn Of The Republic • Semper Fidelis • Star Spangled Banner • You're A Grand Old Flag • and more.

00221801 .... $6.95

TV Hits
Over 20 theme songs that everyone knows, including: Brady Bunch • Cheers • (Meet) The Flintstones • Home Improvement • The Jetsons • Northern Exposure • Mr. Ed • The Munsters Theme • Won't You Be My Neighbor • and more fun favorites!

00221805 .... $9.95

Prices, contents, and availability subject to change without notice.

For More Information, See Your Local Music Dealer, Or Write To:

HAL•LEONARD® CORPORATION
7777 W. Bluemound Rd. P.O. Box 13819 Milwaukee, WI 53213